Culinary History of a Pacific Northwest Town
Bellevue, Washington

Suzanne Knauss

Eastside Heritage Center

Bellevue, Washington

Culinary History of a Pacific Northwest Town: Bellevue, Washington

Publisher: Eastside Heritage Center
Bellevue, Washington

First Printing: 2007

Library of Congress Control Number: 2007903433

Library of Congress Cataloguing-in-Publication Data

1. History - Pacific Northwest - Bellevue (Wash.) -- 20th century. 2. Bellevue (Wash.) - Culinary history. 3. Bellevue (Wash.) - Cookery. 4. Bellevue (Wash.) - Social life and customs. 5. Bellevue (Wash.) - Biography 6. Bellevue (Wash.) Japanese American.

ISBN 978-0-9795758-0-8

Photo Credits: Eastside Heritage Center unless otherwise noted
Design: Donna Cutler and Steffen Fanger, Chi Whiz Creations
Editing: Nancy Valaas
Kayli Martin, Chi Whiz Creations

Printed in the USA at Leatherback Publishing, Kirkland, WA

EASTSIDE
HERITAGE
CENTER
Discover. Share. Participate.

4
CULTURE
KING COUNTY LODGING TAX

Contents

This book is dedicated to all those who gathered around the table to create a community and to the food that nourished their aspirations.

Acknowledgements

I am indebted to many who contributed over the past four years to the development of this book. I owe special thanks to those, including some still actively engaged in their culinary professions, who took time out of their busy lives to tell me their stories. I also thank the Eastside Heritage Center. The EHC Board and Executive Director Heather Trescases offered me support and encouragement, and EHC volunteer Mary Ellen Piro generously researched essential dates and photographs.

Diana Schafer Ford's family candy shop helped inspire the book project; Mike Intlekofer's prodigious knowledge of farming history focused that aspect of the book; Barb Williams' understanding of Native American heritage expanded my vision; Megan Carlisle, EHC Archivist, researched perplexing questions and improved photo quality; Nancy Sheets found newspaper articles; Karen Klett gave me good counsel.

Carolyn Marr, archival librarian for the Museum of History and Industry, provided photos and research assistance. Liz Pearl of Leatherback Publishing ensured the book's publication in more ways than one; designers Donna Cutler, Steffen Fanger and Kayli Martin creatively transformed Bellevue's culinary history into book form.

Julie Creighton's cover design captures perfectly the essence of the culinary history that influenced Bellevue's community life and helped transform it. Nancy Valaas donated many hours editing the text and helping me envision it as a whole. Northwest historian, Charles LeWarne's experiences growing up in Bellevue provided important information and contacts; his keen editing sense proved invaluable. Jacqueline Williams, authoritative Northwest food historian, gave encouraging inspiration and suggestions. Text reviewers' and recipe evaluators' names appear in an appendix. I hope they all realize how essential their endeavors were to the project.

I am grateful for encouragement and inspiration from my 94 year-old mother, Evalyn Schooley Summers, my daughters Pamela Rozsa and Janet Larsen, my grandson Reif Thomas Larsen. Always someone close to the writer must lend the moral support to make it happen. My husband, Tom, did that and so much more. His patience and insights meant so much and gave me the courage to achieve my dream. I couldn't have written the book without him.

Preface

Food features in our most treasured memories. We remember birthday cakes and parties, the Thanksgiving turkey and pumpkin pie, and the Fourth of July strawberry shortcake. Almost always food is associated with historical events. I became intrigued with this and wanted to tell those culinary stories. Think of these stories as ingredients in a recipe, each ingredient important to the recipe's success, added one after the other to influence the outcome.

Bellevue's food history is distinctive, partly because its geography contributed bountiful resources. Native Americans came first to Bellevue's shores to fish and forage. Early Bellevue settlers came for the country life and farming. Strawberry and blueberry fields, small farms and dairy cows ambling in pastures along winding streams and picturesque lakes come to mind when we think of Bellevue's early days. Those strawberries gave Bellevue its first identity, with the Strawberry Festival providing an early opportunity for community life.

Bellevue's chronological timeline reflects culinary trends occurring throughout America, but the difference is in the details of Bellevue's story. Bellevue had soda fountains and ice cream parlors, as did other small towns in the 1930's and 1940's, but how did Bellevue, the town, profit from its citizens enjoying Green River sodas and sundaes? Who made the candies and baked the cakes for celebrations, and how did those enterprises shape Bellevue? What do crabapples have to do with the Bellevue Arts Museum and the Kandy Kane Kafe with the Overlake Hospital? How did a young girl's dream to learn the culinary arts bring Julia Child into Bellevue's kitchens? What do these stories reveal about the community?

Cranes and construction have changed Bellevue's landscape and erased landmarks. Gone today are the strawberry fields, crabapple orchards and grape vines, the family-owned candy and bakeshops, the Bellevue Clubhouse, the Main Street Schoolhouse, the little grocery stores and the family-owned drive-in restaurants. Some enterprises endure and continue operating into the twenty-first century: the blueberry farms, Toy's Café, and the Pancake Corral. Other ventures have come and gone; for example, Chez Nancy, Frederick & Nelson and its tearoom, and Farrell's Ice Cream Parlour. Some closed their doors, but their influence remains: DeLaurenti's and imported foods, Paul Thomas Winery and the culture of wine, the Yankee Kitchen Shop and the culinary arts.

What of Bellevue's culinary future? Today, national chain restaurants and hotel grand openings influence Bellevue's culinary story. At the same time, many small, locally owned, mostly ethnic, food shops and cafés are opening on Main Street and outside the downtown corridor, providing a balance to the ubiquitous chains. Moreover, the response to the 2004 opening of the Bellevue Farmers Market may signify the revival of the "heart and soul" of an ostensibly sophisticated big city. In the twenty-first century, what culinary enterprises and events will attract volunteers and leading citizens to come together as a community?

My sources include interviews, diaries, shop records, old and new cookbooks, and newspaper archives. I organized the text by era, including restaurants, shops and institutions I thought to be of interest and a part of the story. I only wish I could have mentioned all of Bellevue's worthy establishments. Neither a restaurant guide nor a recipe book, these stories are meant to encourage the visitor to explore Bellevue and to enjoy its restaurants, food shops, local markets, and remaining farms. I have included heritage recipes with their original wording because they reflect the period, availability of ingredients and tastes of the time. An evaluation team of experienced cooks tested the more contemporary recipes. I enjoyed researching the stories and uncovering all the fascinating facts. Now, especially when I taste a strawberry, I am taken back to Bellevue's past.

Suzanne Knauss
Bellevue, Washington
June, 2007

Forward

"I grew up in Bellevue when it was a somewhat undistinguished small town. I was Charlie Younger's paperboy - and received a bag or two of mints every time I collected. I grew up with annual Strawberry Festivals, made special trips to Jane McDowell's candy shop for Mother's Day presents, ate occasionally at some of the small family eateries - a special treat - and licked ice cream cones from Meta Burrows' drugstore. I ate school lunches that I understood were originally a volunteer community effort. I remember when Carol Barber's Kandy Kane signified that Bellevue business was moving from Main Street to the new Square, and we marveled when our little town acquired The Crabapple, a graceful and tasteful destination restaurant for the East-side and Seattle."

Charles P. LeWarne, Pacific Northwest Historian

Strawberries and Early Community Life 1869 to 1940

Food and Pioneer History

Food: A Native American Measure of Wealth

Native Americans peopled the shores of Puget Sound and its surrounding hills long before other explorers and pioneers arrived in the nineteenth century. The abundance and availability of food allowed them time to develop a rich cultural life. They measured their wealth by their food stores and demonstrated their prosperity to other tribes by entertaining them at feasts in their longhouses.

One tribe, the Hah-Tshu-Ab'sh, or "Lake People," had settlements in the Bellevue area.[1] Plentiful food sources included kokanee salmon from Lake Washington; ducks, deer and elk from forests; berries, ferns, roots, and wild onions from the lowlands. All these sources of food encouraged their trips along the shores of Lake Washington.[2]

They established camps on Yarrow Bay near an area of wetlands and along the Mercer Slough. They came in order to fish; not unlike the Euro-American settlers who later came to Bellevue's shores and built cabins to use as summer retreats. The two cultures crossed in the 1880's when William Meydenbauer and Aaron Mercer staked their claims on Bellevue's shore lands and reported seeing "Lake People" rowing their canoes in the waters bordering Bellevue.[3]

Puget Sound Native American Fish Cookery

Native American Seafood Cookery

Native Americans cooked in fire pits. They wrapped whole fish in seaweed when living in coastal regions, or they used spits supported by a pole rack suspended about two feet over the fire. They also dried fish and berries for use during the long winter months.[4]

Christina Orchid, chef and owner of Christina's on Orcas Island, respects the Northwest Native American culinary tradition of using fresh foods harvested from the land and waters. Although no evidence exists for Northwest tribes cooking on planks, Christina recommends this method to impart the traditional flavor associated with Native American salmon cookery.[5]

Christina's Planked Salmon

Preheat oven to 400 degrees F.
Brush salmon filets with oil and sprinkle with salt.
Place the filets on a cedar plank or a clean shingle.
Roast fish for ten minutes or until the fish separates from the skin and is firm.

Cooking Stove Flue Scraper circa 1925

Food and Picnics in a Pioneer Community

Clarissa Colman lived on a farm she and her husband established in 1875 south of Bellevue. One day, in 1886, her husband took a boat to Seattle where he was to testify in a trial. On the way he was the victim of an unsolved murder. From that time, Clarissa began writing down her story, using pen and ink, in large, leather-bound journals. She wrote every day for twenty-four years until her death in 1910, providing details of early life on the Eastside.

Clarissa and her sons lived off their land, selling butter and other farm products to neighbors and to the mining store located nearby at the Newcastle coal mines. Food they grew and preserved sustained them and connected them with neighboring pioneer families who were also isolated on farms. Many of these farms were only accessible by boat or by traveling rough, unpaved roads on horseback. The Colmans lived near the eastern shores of Lake Washington south of Bellevue. Boaters landed frequently and visited the Colman farm where they picnicked alongside a nearby creek. Clarissa apparently provided lunch; it could be said that she had the first food concession on the Eastside.[6]

Clarissa Colman gives a few details about her pioneer kitchen. For cooking and baking, Clarissa used a cast iron coal and wood-fired stove. She notes that she had to blacken it, and she would have used a flue scraper to clean the flues inside its firebox.

Excerpts from the Colman Diaries

1901

May 6 - Hard frost. Pleasant day. Done washing. Elaina was in a while brought me some rhubarb from the ranch.

July 10 - Cloudy as usual. Rained quite hard and quite a while tonight after 8 o'clock. George took 3 orlls [sic] butter* up to the Dutchman to sell at Newcastle.

July 26 - Cloudy nearly all day. Very poor hay weather.

August 18 - made 6 glasses of apple jelly.

August 2 - put some apples to dry.

August 2 - George went down to Turners and sold some plums.

September 10 - George began digging potatoes by the grove.

1902

May 8 - I baked bread today. Have been doing some of the kitchen work for several days. George sowed his oats today.

May 12 - George began plowing the ground in the meadow for beets.

August 3 - A naftha [sic] launch landed and put off eleven people. . . .at noon who went down to the creek for lunch. Soon after two men came and got lunch. . .Just as the first party left a boat load of five young fellows landed and went toward creek but soon returned and they got lunch.**

*Pioneer families who had a cow prospered. With a ready supply of milk, they made their own butter and used it for barter or to sell. They formed it in rolls and found it to be superior to store butter, the latter known as "pickle roll" butter and preserved in brine, resulting in a very salty product.[7]

**It seems that "lunch" may have more the idea of light refreshments, sandwiches, cookies or cake and coffee. It is not clear, but presumably Clarissa charged for these lunches. A Naptha-fueled vessel brought these people across Lake Washington to Clarissa's farm site.[8]

William Meydenbauer: Seattle Baker Makes Bellevue History

In 1869 two Bellevue pioneers filed land claims on the eastern shores of Lake Washington. Aaron Mercer staked a claim along Mercer Slough.[9] William Meydenbauer, owner of the Eureka Bakery in Seattle, took up his eighty-acre claim on the marshy shores of what later became known as Meydenbauer Bay.[10] He built a cabin there, and records indicate the family came to hunt, fish, and enjoy the beautiful surroundings. One of the earliest photos of Bellevue shows the Meydenbauers having a picnic there.[11]

He eventually sold off the Meydenbauer Bay property and in 1906 built a summer cabin on Hunts Point. His Seattle bakery, located at Third and Columbia, produced European candies, cookies and holiday cakes for early settlers who were otherwise limited to homemade gingerbread and apples. His bakery had other specialties, including cream puffs and Boston brown bread sold with a crock of baked beans. Meydenbauer owned and operated the Eureka bakery from 1868 to 1890; in 1897, his eldest son, Albert, re-established the bakery at the same location. For Christmas, Meydenbauer made Stollen with almond paste and baked honey cake, or Lebkuchen, in long pans, cut while still warm into 3-inch by 5-inch pieces and packaged. A package of six sold for five cents. For Lebkuchen he used *Hounihan's Bakers' and Confectioners' Guide* that had as its first instruction: "Put five pounds of strained honey in a basin, place on the fire and let it come to a boil. . . ."[12]

Heritage Recipe
German Lebkuchen

4 ounces unsalted butter

6 ounces sugar

1 package vanilla sugar (found in import or German food stores) or 1 teaspoon
   vanilla

1 egg

1 egg yolk

3/4 cup honey

1/2 teaspoon ground anise seed

1 teaspoon ground cloves

1 teaspoon cinnamon

4 cups flour

3 teaspoons baking powder

3 teaspoons milk

Preheat the oven to 350 degrees F.

Cream butter and gradually add all ingredients except for the last three. Mix 2/3 of
the flour with the baking powder and add to the butter mixture, alternating with the
milk. Add the remaining flour and knead until well integrated. If the dough is a bit
sticky, refrigerate for a while.

Roll out on floured board to a 1/4 inch thickness or less. Cut into traditional rectangles
or use cookie cutters to cut out shapes. Bake on a greased cookie sheet for about 10
minutes. Do not overbake.

Glaze

Mix 2 cups of confectioner's sugar with 1 egg white and 2 teaspoons lemon juice until
well combined. Spread over slightly cooled cookies. At this time, the Lebkuchen can be
decorated with sprinkles or sliced almonds, if desired.[13]

Yield: 2 dozen 3 inch by 5 inch pieces

Bellevue Dining for the Whaling Ship Crews

After the July 4, 1917, dedication of the Ship Canal and the Hiram M. Chittenden
Locks to link Lake Washington and Puget Sound, the American Pacific Whaling Co.
(1919-1942) brought its ships into Lake Washington for the winter, docking below 99th
Avenue NE and Bellevue's Main Street.[14]

Mrs. Carter's Boarding House

The whaling crew dined at Mrs. Florence Carter's Bellevue boarding house. Mrs. Carter fed the boisterous crew in the kitchen. More genteel diners, including longtime Bellevue residents, Don Johnson's uncle and his wife, sat at linen-covered tables in the dining room.[15] Mrs. Carter served "Plate Meals" advertised for 35 cents. Plate meals might have featured meat pies, croquettes with gravy, fried chicken, scalloped liver or creamed oysters and molded jello.[16] In 2007, an antique business occupies the former boarding house. The boarding house, Main Street's oldest structure, is located on an alley just south of Main Street and west of 102nd Avenue NE.

Dances and Picnics on Meydenbauer Bay

Harry Cade and Louis Carlson purchased a steamboat they christened the Wild-

wood. They advertised boat excursions from Seattle to the Meydenbauer Bay dock for dancing and liquid refreshments, parties and picnics at the park and hall they named for their boat. From 1906 until the 1920's, the population gathered for weekend events at Wildwood Park on Meydenbauer Bay where there was a band shell and dance floor.[17] The Fraternal Order of Hawks, an African American organization in Seattle, held its annual August picnic in Bellevue. They

Wildwood Pavilion circa 1910

took along picnic lunches and rode the ferry from Leschi Park, departing in the morning and spending all day on Bellevue's shores where they played baseball, listened to band music and danced.[18]

Joseph Kardong visited relatives in Seattle in 1910 and attended a basket social at Wildwood Park. He returned in 1916 with his Minnesota family and later opened a store in Bellevue's Midlakes area.[19]

From 1918 to 1920, the Henry Wegners operated the Wildwood lunchroom in a 1902 house built next to the ferry landing. Also at the landing, Grace Sandell operated the Bellevue Lunch and Confectionery. When in 1920 the ferries no longer stopped at the Meydenbauer landing, the Wegners moved the house to Main Street where they

served special dinners. In 1928, they sold their business to R.J. Orth.[20]

The "Grubstake"

In the early 1900's, anyone living in Bellevue depended on boat transportation. Even groceries arrived by a boat, called the "Grubstake," that a firm by the name of Augustine & Kyer, a Seattle specialty grocery, supplied. A floating grocery on a powered scow, the Grubstake made the rounds, stopping at little Bel-

Grubstake Grocery Boat circa 1910

levue communities located on Lake Washington. Residents signaled the boat with a white flag to indicate they needed supplies. "Getting seasick while shopping on a rough day was not uncommon," recalled Beaux Arts' resident James Ditty in an interview for the October 27, 1958, *Bellevue American*.

Provisions and First Friends

Where in Bellevue did early settlers shop and what did they purchase? Bellevue's rural landscape in the early 1900's created a patchwork of fields cleared of fir forests,

Medina General Store circa 1920

crossed by dirt roads and, by 1904, cut by the Northern Pacific Railroad line running north and south through what became known as the Midlakes. Those who settled in Bellevue and others who only came for the summer became acquainted when they shopped for provisions either on Main Street in the Midlakes area, or in unincorporated Medina. Grocery stores became gathering places.

Main Street, known then as St. James Road, linked Bellevue's rural population with ferry landings on Meydenbauer Bay, Clyde Beach and Medina. In 1908, Patrick McGauvran opened Main Street's first business, the Bellevue Mercantile, where he sold groceries and general goods. The Bellevue Mercantile Company store supplied residents with groceries, hardware, grain and flour. Long-time residents remembered it as "a genuine old-fashioned place with open barrels of peanut butter and crackers and all other things that were needed in this remote area."[21]

Walt Hagerstein built the Medina store in 1908. He hung a hook to display bananas and installed a cookie and cake stand. The store sold Swift's Premium hams and bacon and advertised ice cream Sundays [sic]. The Medina store has remained in operation for almost one hundred years under various owners and will reopen in 2007 with new ownership and extensive renovation. In the late twentieth century, as in its early years, the store served as a meeting place for adults, a place where children in the neighborhood could go on their own with pocket change to buy candy or ice cream.[22]

Several stores opened in the Midlakes area near the railroad tracks where they received railroad carloads of goods for their customers. In 1920, Joseph Kardong operated a store there and advertised coffee at 32 cents a pound, canned pink salmon at 13 cents a can or two for 25 cents, and a "Full line of LeHuquet's Reliable Extracts." Customers went there to buy alfalfa and timothy hay by the ton and could have their groceries delivered free with the purchase of feed. They had their horses shoed next door. In fact, Joseph Kardong's first store burned to the ground, perhaps because of a fire started in the adjoining blacksmith's shop.[23]

Early Food Industries

Fisher Flouring Mills officially opened June 1, 1911, on Harbor Island in Elliott Bay. The Fishers, who later founded a radio station (KOMO), ran the flourmill until 2001 when they sold it to Pendleton Flour Mills.[24] Newspapers, including *The Lake Washington Reflector*, published in Bellevue, began printing recipes referring to the new brands of cooking products available to the home cook: Fisher's Flour, Spry and Crisco vegetable shortening, Kerr Mason jars for canning. The new commercial products influenced the development of recipes.

Fisher Mills Recipe Pamphlet circa 1923 [25]

Farms, Festivals and the Fruit and Flower Mission

Heart of the Charmed Land

The rolling contours of the land indented by the many bays of Lake Washington dotted with other lakes, hills and valleys lend their enchantment of varied vistas. The Olympics, Cascades and Mt. Rainier are visible from most every part of the district. This 1927 portrayal of Bellevue, Washington, describes the district as the "heart of the charmed land" famous for strawberries, grapes, lettuce, tomatoes, peas, corn, cherries, berries, pears, apples, poultry, rabbits, bulbs, flowers, ornamental shrubbery and dairies.[26]

Joe's Place Advertisement circa 1930

According to farming enthusiast, Mike Intlekofer, Bellevue had some traits that made it a very special place for agriculture. Due to its temperate climate and diverse topography, settlers could grow a large variety of plants and raise livestock in and around Bellevue. Valley bottoms, hillsides and wetlands, all proved to be ideal for some type of crop.[27]

In addition, farmers, because of their diligence and ingenuity, produced great yields. The Aries Brothers' farm in the Larsen Lake area shipped the first carload of iceberg lettuce, and by 1917 was transporting carloads of lettuce across the country. They layered hand-chipped ice between the heads for shipping. In 1932, Tom Matsuoka helped found the Bellevue Vegetable Growers Association, and it shipped under the Belle-View label as many as 50 boxcars in a season, full of fruit and vegetables destined for points as distant as New York, Alaska and Hawaii.[28]

Most farms produced two crops a year, and farmers maximized yields using greenhouses. In 1942, farmers raised greenhouse crops of cucumbers, tomatoes, chrysanthemums, Easter lilies and geraniums. Although there was a diversity of crops, Bellevue's signature crop before World War II was the strawberry. Acres in and around Bellevue were dedicated to this important delicacy. In the 1950's, blueberries became Bellevue's farm crop of choice, and annual harvests produced as many as 350,000 pounds.[29]

Clearing the Land

In 1878, David Shiach planted the first of the town's orchards between 100th Avenue NE and 108th Avenue NE in Bellevue. In 1892, Dr. Charles M. Martin purchased 100 acres at NE 4th and 108th Avenue NE to cultivate fruit trees. When he moved to his Bellevue property, he became the town's first physician.[30] The Homestead Act of 1893 encouraged settlement of the large tracts east of Seattle, across Lake Washington. As settlers bought up property on the Eastside, they hired Japanese laborers to do the backbreaking work of logging and clearing the land, as well as farming it.

Mickleson Family Making Cider circa 1935

Visiting Bellevue's Agricultural Past

Even today, travel around the various residential and commercial areas of Bellevue almost always reveals something of its agricultural past. In 1880, Patrick Downey claimed land on Clyde Hill, and in the early 1900's cultivated 15 acres of strawberries there. His property, still referred to as Downey Hill, encompassed the land that became the Vuecrest development off 100th Avenue NE in downtown Bellevue.[31]

In 1902, Edward Tremper used a horse and plow to plant holly imported from England on Yarrow Point acreage in unincorporated west Bellevue. English holly takes

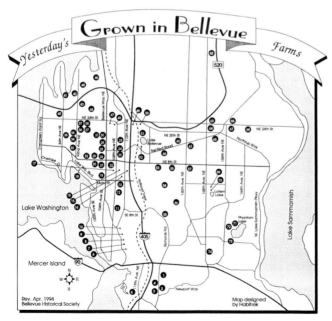

Pre-World War II Bellevue Farm Map

ten to twelve years to mature, so as an alternative crop, Tremper planted strawberry plants between the rows of holly. By 1920 he could harvest the holly, and for the harvesting and shipping employed as many as thirty workers. They took the cut holly in boxes to the Bellevue Postmistress, Adelaide Belote, who shipped the Christmas wreaths all over the country.[32]

In 1905, John Siepmann bought 60 acres off of 148th Avenue NE and NE 24th in the Highland area. Siepmann's son, George, later started the Highland Dairy. In 1923, on 190 acres east of the town, the W. H. Duey Family began to build barns for what became known as the Twin Valley Dairy. The dairy land eventually became Kelsey Creek Park. The City of Bellevue moved the 1888 Fraser Cabin from its original Northup site to the park. These surviving buildings, which are open to the public, provide evidence of Bellevue's early agricultural history.[33]

The Balaticos farmed along the Mercer Slough from 1945 to the 1980's. They had a popular vegetable stand where they sold fresh peas, corn, beans, carrots and zucchini, and everyone went to their fields in the fall to find a pumpkin to carve for Halloween.[34] For over fifty years from 1950 until 2000, John Matsuoka farmed 2.75 acres located at the southeast corner of 156th Avenue and SE 16th Street in the Lake Hills Greenbelt in Bellevue. He grew lettuces, brussel sprouts, potatoes and corn. His famous sweet Silver Queen corn earned him the title of the "Corn King" of Bellevue. After he retired, he donated time teaching about farming to schoolchildren.[35] Laotian Toulue Cha continues to operate a sales stand for vegetables and flowers they cultivate near the Lake Hills Ranger station at 156th Ave NE on land owned by the City of Bellevue.

Strawberry Cultivation

Pioneers who settled in and around Bellevue, had not gone into full-scale cultivation of strawberry plants as a crop. In 1904, Sakutaro Takami planted the first recorded patch of strawberries at 102nd NE and NE 15th in Bellevue. When Japanese immigrants arrived, they recognized that they would not be in competition with other farmers if they cultivated strawberries.[36] As a result, they became the principal farmers for the acres of strawberries that gave Bellevue agricultural fame. By the 1920's, the Japanese leased or owned many of the berry and truck farms that by then covered much of Bellevue. They grew acres of the Marshall strawberry, prized for its flavor.

Airmail Stamp 1938

In 1923 Henry Fisher, owner of the new Kirkland canning company, learned about a strawberry developed by crossing the Marshall and Clark berries. He encouraged growers to grow the "Ettersburg-121" berry, because it yielded 400 to 500 crates of berries per acre and proved to be more uniform and better for shipping and canning. In 1932, Japanese farmers founded the Bellevue Vegetable Growers Association, a cooperative venture with a warehouse and packing house alongside the Northern Pacific railway tracks off of NE 8th. They shipped snap beans, celery, cucumbers and strawberries under the Belle-View label.[37]

Mitzie (Takeshita) Hashiguchi's family lived on a 13-acre farm in the "Midlake Row" section of Bellevue, not far from Bellevue Lake. "We had acres and acres of strawberries, and grew our own vegetables too," recalled Mitzie.[38] "We only put strawberries on the cake. Japanese didn't use cream or eat cheese for a long time, in my family, not until we got a Norwegian daughter-in-law!" Mitzie contributed her mother's strawberry recipes.

Heritage Recipe
Strawberry Farm Jam

Kuma Takeshita
Wash, hull and slice 5 cups strawberries.
Add 2 cups sugar, stirring well.
Bring mixture to a boil and cook for one minute.
Store in clean jars and put in the greenhouse for two days or until thickened.

The Strawberry Festival Unites the Community

The Strawberry Festival, inaugurated on the grounds of the old school house at the west end of Main Street, was a major factor in the development of the entire Eastside.

It "literally put Bellevue 'on the map.'"[39]

By 1925, Bellevue had become so famous for its berries, that it inaugurated its first Strawberry Festival. Jenny and Charles W. Bovee, along with Mr. William Cruse, originated the idea to honor Bellevue's bountiful straw-

Strawberry Festival circa 1930   berry crops.[40] The Japanese

farmers and other growers donated the strawberries, and volunteers baked the shortcakes. The first year, 3,000 visitors attended the fair. They held the first festival in June at the school on Main Street, and in subsequent years on the Bellevue Clubhouse grounds, where festival visitors ate their shortcakes and enjoyed watching skits and acts performed on a stage.

In 1925 and 1926, ladies from the Bellevue Woman's Club mixed the festival shortcakes in their home kitchens and baked them in the high school oven, then fired with coal. They served more than 2000 visitors. By 1927, due to the festival's increasing popularity, Fisher Flouring Mills offered the use of its electric ovens and their staff to make the shortcakes, 6,000 that year.[41] By 1938, approximately 15,000 attended the festival, consuming 4,172 pounds of strawberries, 69 gallons of whipping cream, 100 gallons of ice cream and 8,750 shortcakes.[42] The start of World War II, the shortage of sugar and in 1942, the internment of the Japanese-Americans who farmed the strawberries, ended the celebration of the festival.

Bellevue Blueberries

In 1933, W. B. Sydnor planted the first five acres of blueberries in Bellevue off 106th Avenue NE on land occupied today by the Barnes and Noble Bookstore. Blueberry cultivation continues to thrive in Bellevue since W. B. Sydnor planted those first acres of blueberries. In the 1940's Louis Weinzirl acquired 16 acres in the wetlands located east of 148th Avenue SE and north of SE 8th, an area including Larsen Lake and known for its wild huckleberries. There, he planted domestic blueberry

Sydnor's Blueberry Label circa 1935

plants that eventually numbered 9,000 bushes.[43] In 1947, Lee Dennison planted 25 acres of blueberries along the Mercer Slough south of Bellevue's Main Street, establishing the Overlake Blueberry Farm. Currently, the Natural Resources Division of Bellevue oversees the 14-acre Larsen Lake blueberry farm as well as the Mercer Slough Blueberry Farm. [44]

The Mercer Slough farm's 18,000 bushes produce annually an average of 100 tons of blueberries. Bill Pace became its operations manager in 2001. He is proud of the increasing blueberry yields that provide a ready source of fresh blueberries for Bellevue's residents and some commercial establishments he sells to, including Whole Foods. They grow Jersey, Weymouth, Bluecrop, Rancocca and a Concord-Rubel Mix variety of blueberries. U-Pick customers and farm workers handpick all the berries, because picking machines can't operate on the farm's rich, but unstable, marshland, created in 1916 when the Chittenden Locks in Ballard lowered Lake Washington.[45]

Farmed Blueberries

"Like many people raised in the Pacific Northwest, my earliest memories of food revolve around farm-raised fruits and vegetables. As a child growing up in the Seattle area, I often accompanied my mother to her favorite garden market at the Overlake Blueberry Farm in Bellevue, where the scents, sounds, and sights of the lively market enveloped my senses. It was there that I learned the secrets

BLUEBERRY BUCKLE

Cream: ½ cup Sugar and ½ cup Shortening and add 1 beaten Egg.
Sift: 2 cups Flour.
　　¼ teasp. Salt.
　　2½ teasp. Baking Powder and add to above creamed mixture alternately with 2/3 cup of milk and add ½ teasp. Lemon Extract. Pour into well greased 8" cake pan and sprinkle 1 cup Blueberries over batter.
Mix: ½ cup sugar
　　½ teasp. cinnamon
　　½ cup flour (scant)
　　¼ cup butter and sprinkle this mixture over berries, bake at 350° for 45 minutes.

Sydnor's Blueberry Buckle recipe circa 1935

of selecting produce - of picking only fruits and vegetables that sparkled with life, heavy with the sensual weight of ripeness, and that exuded the quintessential aroma produce exudes only when it has attained perfection." Lori McKean.[46]

Fruit and Flower Mission and Overlake Service League

In 1911, before electricity had reached all of Bellevue, a group of women founded the Hunts Point Circle of Seattle's Fruit and Flower Mission, an organization dedi-

cated to providing milk and clothing for poor Seattle children. These founding members lived in Seattle during the winter and came by boat with their provisions and children across Lake Washington to summer homes on Hunts Point. In the early years of the Circle's existence, mem-

Fruit & Flower Mission circa 1911

bers gathered over tea and cookies to sew layettes for newborns and plan fundraising events; they supported Red Cross efforts during the Depression and the war years. In October 1918, *The Lake Washington Reflector* articles reported, "The Fruit and Flower will do Belgian Relief Work every Tuesday at Mrs. Bilger's home; on November 1st," the newspaper recorded, "Fruit and Flower built 200 'flu' masks last Tuesday."[48] See "Community Support for Lunch Programs" on page 48.

Cooking Demonstrations

In 1922, rummage sales and bridge parties raised funds for their projects. They also sponsored cooking demonstration classes. "Mrs. Coo demonstrated rolls and potato muffins; Mrs. Fisher, coffee cake, cheese pastry, snow balls, hazel nut cake and cinnamon rolls."[49] Mrs. Fisher's recipe for steamed snow balls disappeared from cookbooks printed after the 1950's.

Tea in Delkin's Bulb Room

As the Eastside's population grew, members joined the Fruit and Flower Mission from several communities, and by 1928 the Hunts Point Circle divided into three groups, Hunts Point, Medina-Evergreen and Bellevue, referred to as the Overlake Circle of the Fruit and Flower Mission. In 1929 the groups started a tearoom in Mrs. Delkin's bulb room to raise funds for their projects. Fred Delkin's bulb business represented one of Bellevue's earliest industries.[50]

The Overlake Service League replaced the Overlake Circle in 1935, providing centralized organization for smaller community-based circles. Circles sponsored fundraising for Bellevue projects: scholarships, holiday food baskets, family counseling and funds to provide school supplies and clothing for school children.[51]

Confections and Community Connections

Home Entertainments

William and Mary Cruse with their daughter, Grace Catherine, came to Seattle from Ohio, arriving in June of 1889 just before Washington became a state and during the great Seattle fire that destroyed most of the city. In 1910 Grace Catherine Cruse married Climie Eugene Hill. Hill wanted to move to Bellevue and be a "gentleman farmer." He and Grace purchased Pastor Baker's house, property that became the site for the Bellevue Village QFC grocery store.

Hill Family Children's Tea Party circa 1919

Typical of rural community life in the early 1900's, the Hills usually had a house full of guests - relatives, boarders and friends. The Hills did all their own cooking and baking and made their own home entertainments. Grace Hill made two pies a day, meat turnover pies as well as fruit pies. They always enjoyed music - Grace often acted as accompanist - and they especially enjoyed performing and dramatizing musical selections in costume. The family history notes that their only child Mary Phyllis Hill Fenwick (1913 - 2004) recited poetry at these home entertainments.[52]

Bellevue and Highland Community Centers

Box Socials

The community celebrated events in the Bellevue Clubhouse, located two blocks north of Main Street, after its construction in 1915. In 1921, *The Lake Washington Reflector* newspaper reported that Phyllis Hill and thirty friends gathered at the Bellevue Club for her eighth birthday, celebrated as a Valentine's Party on Saturday, February 5th, with "dainty refreshments and musical games" to entertain the guests. In the 1920's and 1930's, the community celebrated the Strawberry Festival there.[53]

Bellevue Clubhouse

As early as 1910, residents of the Highland district met for meetings in local homes and the Northup School House for box socials, dancing, housewarmings, debates and recitations. Since the days of the one-room school house, box socials provided both a social and a fundraising event. Ladies decorated boxes with ribbon and fabric or paper and made sure to pack a delicious lunch inside the box with sandwiches or fried chicken and always dessert. The auctioning off of the boxes heightened the excitement of the crowd waiting to see who would be partners to share each fancy box. In 1910, the Highland Community Club sponsored a box social, presumably to help finance a new clubhouse, at the Northup Schoolhouse on the evening of November 16th. The Highland Community Club also contributed to Bellevue's Strawberry Festival.[54] In 1938, with the help of the WPA program, members of the Highland Community Club constructed a new clubhouse, near the intersection of 24th and 140th NE, a distinctive log structure in use today.[55]

The Wake Robin Lodge: Chicken Dinner and a "Day in the Country"

The February 20, 1927, issue of *The Lake Washington Reflector* announced that "A. Cunningham and C. James of Seattle have taken over the S. Krueger place at Enatai on a long time lease and after extensive improvements opened it under the name of Wake Robin Lodge on Saturday, Feb. 19. Chicken dinners, private dining rooms and specialty catering with good music is the order of this new local institution. . ."[56] Located in a beautiful setting with a view to the east, the lodge's main building featured an enormous stone fireplace and balconies.

The Cunninghams and James, as owners of the first African-American business on the east side of Lake Washington, created a popular destination for bridge parties, teas, lunch and dinner, and not only for local residents. People drove around Lake Washington or took a ferry and came to the lodge to eat their chicken dinners with fresh vegetables and to spend "a day in the country." According to Leila Cook Martin and her brother, William B. Cook, who grew up next-door, the lodge was self-sufficient with long chicken coops, a small dairy, a garden and an orchard. Bill Cook remembers the two families. The Cunninghams "were the ruling faction that drove a shiny, quiet Nash with wooden spoke wheels at a sedate pace on the long driveway in and out of the Lodge. . . Mr. Jones tended the chicken ranch which consisted of a number of chicken houses where they raised white leghorns that he protected from the Great Horned Owls and Red Tail Hawks with an awesome shotgun leaning against the wall. . . "[57]

The high school class of 1933 celebrated its Junior-Senior Banquet there as did other large groups who came for parties and to dance on its beautiful hardwood floors.[58] The continuing effects of the Depression eventually forced the lodge to close, and by 1941 much of the original building had fallen into ruin.

Bellevue Candy Shops

The McDowell Candy Shop

Jane McDowell Candy Shop circa 1930

Fran Bigelow, founder of internationally renowned Fran's Chocolates, credits her passion for chocolate to Seattle's 1940's and 1950's small candy shops where "quality and hand-craftsmanship were prized."[59] During this era, notable were the McDowell Candy Shop located at what is now 17th and Bellevue Way, and Younger's Mints on Main Street.

The practice of offering a box of fancy chocolates on special occasions became a part of Bellevue's culinary tradition with the arrival of home candy-making enterprises. The McDowell Candy Shop and Younger's Mints both contributed their tantalizingly fresh confections to the increasingly sophisticated social customs of the small town.

World War II Sugar Rationing Coupon

Now citizens could purchase candies for Mother's Day and holidays. During World War II to maintain their tradition of giving candy as gifts, many in Bellevue donated their sugar ration coupons to Mina McDowell Schafer, so she could continue to operate her business in spite of wartime shortages.

Home candy making had become a passion for Mina (Elmina) McDowell Schafer who experimented with a recipe until she created it perfectly. Mina Schafer opened the Jane McDowell Candy Shop at NE 20th on Bellevue Way during the Depression in 1930, naming it after her mother, Jennie (Jane) McDowell. She sold her famous candies first from her house on the hill and later from the quaint cottage complete with fireplace that her husband, Louis Schafer, built below the house. In the early days, a bell system connected the house and cottage so customers could alert her when they arrived to buy candy. Before bridges crossed the lake, Mina either took the ferry across Lake Washington or drove around the lake to purchase candy-making supplies in Seattle.

Jane McDowell Candy Shop

Louis also helped her create the butter mints and the peanut brittle, so she could concentrate on making fondant and hand-dipping the chocolates. All of her family helped in the business including her daughter, Marguerite Eminson; her daughter-in-law, Violet Schafer; and later her granddaughter, Diana Schafer Ford, who has preserved her grandmother's recipes and remembers her candy making techniques.

Diana believes using the best ingredients: whipping cream, butter and fresh nuts, made her grandmother's candies so delicious, and she remembers going with her to buy freshly roasted nuts at Buddy Squirrels in Seattle.

At Christmas, Mina's popular candies were shipped to such notables as President Roosevelt and Chuck Connors. Mina Schafer sold her shop in 1952 to Ina and Ben Johnson who called it the Kandy Kottage. Mina continued to work there for a few years.[60]

Mina McDowell Shafer Family Recipes

Recipes for homemade candies require skill and dedication. Nevertheless, it can be satisfying to create a simplified version of fondant to stuff into dates or figs and to make chocolate truffles to tuck into holiday gift boxes. Recipes requiring special equipment and expertise we list as heritage recipes and recommend only for those who have patience and experience.

Heritage Recipe
Fondant
Mina McDowell Schafer

Mina's Fondant became her signature candy, and the recipe she, alone, mastered. Use cooked fondant as the basis for candy creams or, thinned with sugar syrup, pour it over cakes.

3 cups sugar
1/4 cup corn syrup
1/4 teaspoon salt
1 teaspoon glycerin
1/2 pint (1 cup) heavy cream or half and half

Blend sugar, cream of tartar, corn syrup, glycerin, cream and salt in a two-quart saucepan. Cook over moderate heat to boiling. Cover pan. Boil mixture two to three minutes.

Uncover and wipe down any crystals from the sides of the pan, using a cloth moistened with hot water. Boil until mixture reaches 236° (soft-ball stage).
Dampen marble slab with water and pour on fondant. When candy has cooled, work in butter and flavoring using two candy spatulas or paddles. ("work" by lifting and folding the mixture from the edges to the center until it becomes opaque and creamy)

Cover with a damp cloth until ready to use.

Roll into rods and cut into round or oval shapes and dip in chocolate.
Melt 1 pound of desired chocolate. Cool chocolate to 88 degrees F and dip candy centers that should be about 70 degrees F, lifting them onto a rack to dry.
Yield: About 1 1/4 pounds

Tested
Chocolate Truffles
Diana Schafer Ford

These truffles are very smooth and creamy with a good dark chocolate flavor. Serve them on a pretty plate and with coffee.

1 cup heavy cream
2/3 cup sugar
12 tablespoons butter
12 ounce package semi-sweet chocolate chips
2 teaspoons vanilla

Combine first 3 ingredients and bring to boil. Remove from heat, immediately add chocolate chips and stir until melted. Add vanilla. Pour into bowl and cool. Chill over night. The next day make a mixture of chocolate powder and place in dish. For the powder, mix 3/4 cup Hershey Cocoa with a few tablespoons of Swiss Mocha powder*. Spoon truffles into balls quickly as it melts fast and roll in chocolate powder. Keep cool until you serve.
Yield: 2 pounds

*Swiss Mocha powder is an instant coffee mix available in supermarkets.
Note: Truffles taste best consumed the first day or two or can be refrigerated.

Younger's Mints

Friends admired Charlie Younger and his mother for their candy-making skills, and by 1926 were coming regularly to purchase their confections made in the basement family home candy kitchen. Often they made mint flavored taffy, and once his mother added too much butter, accidentally creating their trademark "melt in your mouth" Younger's Mints. By 1931, the mints had become so popular that Charlie and his wife moved what had, by then, become a full-time business into the McKee building on Main Street in Bellevue.

Younger's Mints circa 1931

The family preferred keeping the business small in order to maintain quality, but soon the distinctive cans of mints shipped outside the State of Washington. They eventually hired Delbert Hutchison who worked for them fourteen years as candy maker. They moved the candy making and retail business to larger quarters on 104th Avenue

NE in Bellevue. The Youngers finally sold their business in 1947 to George and Mildred Anderson who in 1952 sold to the competing Vernell's Fine Candies, a fully automated operation.[61]

Heritage Recipe
Younger's Mints

8 pounds sugar
1 teaspoon salt
1 ounce syrup
2 1/2 pints boiling water

When candy starts to boil, stir in one ounce of butter. When it reaches 240 degrees F, add 2 ounces more. Cook to 268 degrees F in cold weather and about 274 degrees F in hot weather. Pour onto a marble slab, cool, pull and cut. Flavor with one teaspoon of vanilla and one teaspoon of mint oil - less mint if too strong.

Main Street: Sodas and Cookbooks

Originally, a town of isolated farms, summer places and cottage industries, Bel-

levue soon developed a commercial district on Main Street. People went there to shop and to take their Model T's and Ford trucks to Stennett's gas station on the SE corner of Main and 104th, now called Bellevue Way.

Charles LeWarne, Northwest historian, grew up in Bellevue where his father became postmas-

Main Street circa 1930

ter in 1917 and, later, owned a variety store on Bellevue's Main Street from the late thirties until the mid-1950's. The store, converted to an Italian restaurant today, featured household items, dry goods, stationery, toys, and a center counter candy display. The City of Paris building also survives today. It served as an important gathering place in the early days as the location for Meta Burrows' Lakeside Drug and soda fountain. Downstairs LeWarne remembers folding special edition Wednesday papers to help Al and Elinor Whitney distribute the *Bellevue American* they edited and printed from 1935 to 1952.[62]

Plotting the Future over Sodas and Cinnamon Rolls

In 1934, Meta Burrows opened Lakeside Drug on Main Street and 102nd. Soon community leaders frequented it, gathering around her soda fountain to plan for Bellevue's future. When the drugstore closed in 1979, Paul Vander Hoek was quoted in a news tribute to Burrows, "I'll never forget the buttered cinnamon rolls and Green Rivers. Many early projects in Bellevue were plotted over those cinnamon rolls."[63] Long-time resident Mary Barton recalled that in the 1940's and 1950's everyone went for prescriptions and for a soda at Meta Burrow's Lakeside Drug. "All the businessmen met there," she remembers.[64]

Meta Burrows' Soda Fountain circa 1940

Annie Stevenson worked at Meta's soda fountain. "There really wasn't any recipe for sundaes and floats other than putting ice cream in the dish and covering it with whatever they asked for - nuts, cherry, whipped cream. Floats were about the same - ice cream and pour root beer over the top."[65]

Teachers' Cookies Create Good Will

Bellevue's growing population demanded schools. In 1892, Bellevue built, at the cost of $1500, the two-room Main Street School with a bell tower on the southeast corner of 100th and Main Street.[66]

The five siblings of Mitzie (Takeshita) Hashiguchi attended Hurley Baunsgard's classes. Baunsgard became more than a teacher to the Takeshita family. She kept in touch with the Japanese-American families after they were interned during World War II, and Mitzie remembers with affection her generosity and help after the war. "She was our Santa Claus." Every Christmas, Hurley Baunsgard brought them holiday decorations and toys, dolls and doll buggies for the girls, and once a quilt for her mother. Baunsgard also became known for her home-baked cookies.[67]

When Patricia Sandbo taught in the Bellevue Grade School from 1941 to 1942, her former third-grade teacher, Irene Rudolph, became her teaching colleague. She remembers admiring how Rudolph had a "special way" with the children. Some of Sandbo's Japanese-American students left for internment camps during World War II, and she has kept letters they wrote her during that difficult time. She returned to teaching from 1957 to 1962 with classes at Bellevue Elementary and Hillaire Elementary. She, too, baked cookies with children and remembers how appreciative the children were of everything. "Simple pleasures were enjoyed, and teachers had a close relationship with the parents."[68]

Tested
Heritage Recipe
Peanut Butter Cookies
Hurley Baunsgard

Recipe found in Charles LeWarne's mother's recipe box. Hurley was a close family friend and LeWarne's first grade teacher.
1/2 cup white sugar
1/2 cup brown sugar
1/2 cup shortening or unsalted butter
1 egg
1/2 cup peanut butter, smooth or crunchy
1 teaspoon soda
1 cup flour

Preheat oven to 350 degrees F.
Cream together with an electric mixer the sugars, shortening or butter (and oil, if desired). Mix in the beaten egg (and vanilla if desired). Beat in the peanut butter. Stir together in a separate bowl the soda (or soda and salt, if desired) and flour and add to sugar mixture. Mix until all ingredients are incorporated.
Refrigerate dough for 15 minutes, or until slightly firm. Make teaspoons of the dough into small balls and press flat with fork (dipped in sugar, if desired). Bake in upper third of the oven for 9 to 12 minutes or until light golden brown. Don't overbake. Cool on wire racks and store in an airtight container or freeze.
Yield: 36 2 - inch cookies

Note: Baunsgard's recipe creates a crunchy cookie. To produce a softer, chewier cookie, instead of 1/2 cup shortening or butter, use 6 tablespoons unsalted butter and 1 1/2 tablespoons cooking oil. Some recipes call for 1/2 teaspoon soda and 1/2 teaspoon salt instead of 1 teaspoon soda. Add 1 1/4 teaspoons vanilla to give additional flavor.

Books for Cooks at the Bellevue Public Library

Cookbooks tell history, reflect cultures, relate traditions and systematize the way we cook. In 1896, Fannie Farmer revised the *Boston Cooking School Cook Book* by

standardizing measurements so that the recipes could more reliably be reproduced in the home.[69] In 2005 the Bellevue Regional Library circulated 3500 cookbooks and cooking videos. Cookbooks have become best sellers, even read by people who don't cook, creating top sales figures for bookstores.[70]

January 21, 1932 *The Lake Washington Reflector* announced "Every Housewife Needs Recipe Box" and "A recipe box can be purchased at almost any hardware store,

Marguerite Groves'
Recipe Box circa 1930

book store or gift shop for as little as 50 cents, depending upon how elaborate the box is. No greater satisfaction can come to the homemaker than to have a well organized recipe box filled with her favorite recipes."

Bellevue homemakers may have owned a cookbook or two; most early twentieth century home cooks used recipes handed down from their mothers. In the 1920's, home cooks still prepared most everything. They cured their own hams, made butter and even made home brews.[71] Children of immigrants continued to observe family culinary traditions. In the 1930's, Reda Vander Hoek came to Bellevue with her Dutch family's recipes.

Heritage Recipe
Speculaas Cookies
Reda Vander Hoek

Shape these spicy cookies in a traditional wooden mold or use cookie cutters.
3 cups unsifted flour
1 1/2 teaspoons cinnamon
1 tablespoon ground cloves
1 teaspoon ginger
1/8 teaspoon baking powder
1/2 teaspoon salt
1 cup butter
1 cup brown sugar
1 egg
1/2 cup ground almonds

Preheat oven to 350 degrees F.
Sift flour, baking powder and spices into a bowl. Mix butter brown sugar and eggs until light and fluffy. Stir in half of flour mixture. Mix and add remainder of flour mixture with the ground almonds. Refrigerate in rolls. Shape in the floured mold or cut out and bake 10 to 15 minutes.

Guest Cook

In 1925 the Bellevue Woman's Club opened a lending library with three hundred discards from the Washington State Library along with donations from the Washington State Library and local residents. Jennie Clayton, Marguerite Groves and others, all members of the Bellevue Woman's Club, rotated as volunteer librarians for the small book collection. The library occupied one room of the Bellevue Clubhouse for a time and later moved into a room behind a grocery and café on Main Street. Their collection became the nucleus of the future King County Library System. The King County Library system acquired the Bellevue Library in 1944, and Marguerite Groves became its first paid librarian. The year she retired, on March 26, 1958, the *Bellevue American* made Marguerite Groves its "Guest Cook" and printed her favorite recipe, Snickerdoodle cookies.[72]

Spreading the Culinary News

Newspapers, the repository of new ideas and information, provide a priceless record of food traditions, local taste, and production trends, sometimes contributing to their creation. W. Eugene LeHuquet came to Washington State and, on January 1, 1918, started Bellevue's first weekly newspaper, calling it *The Lake Washington Reflector*. LeHuquet, whose father was a French Canadian from Quebec, grew up in Iowa. He later lived in upper New York where he learned to be a printer. In addition to his journalistic talents, he became proficient as a poet and philatelist, and gained entry three times into the "Ripley's Believe It or Not" records.[73] When he first arrived in Seattle in 1911, he worked in Mr.Graybill's printing office on Yesler Way. During World War I, he decided to publish a paper on the Eastside, printing it for the first ten years in the office on Yesler.

The Lake Washington

REFLECTOR

BELLEVUE   With a Family of 20% Readers in Seattle's Superb Suburbs   /   MEDINA
BEAUX ARTS   ENATIE   FACTORIA   HIGHLAND   HUNT'S POINT   MIDLAKES   WILBURTON   YARROW
Entered as second-class matter Feb. 20, 1918 at the Post Office at Bellevue, Wash., under act of Mar. 3, 1897
Vol. 8 No. 19   BELLEVUE, WASH., U.S.A.   JULY 1, 1925   Whole No. 251

He settled his family at 9616 NE 5th in Bellevue and, in the beginning, conducted business in an office he organized under a tent. When LeHuquet moved the printing operation to Bellevue, he had no linotype and set everything by hand.[74]

Published three times monthly from 1918 to 1934 *The Lake Washington Reflector* provided household hints, recipes, and advertising from local businesses. Its Household Column addressed all issues giving helpful suggestions for how depression-weary consumers could economize as well as what to pack for a picnic. "Meat sandwiches need spicy dressings to make them good. . . Use mustard dressing for ham, gooseberry relish with roast duck, boiled dressing with cold roast beef, horseradish and celery salt with cold roast lamb."[75] For a weekend fishing and camping trip, *The Lake Washington Reflector* columnist wrote, "It's well to go provided against starvation, in case the fish don't bite."[76]

W. Eugene LeHuquet

"My Neighbor Says" appeared as a regular column for homemakers. In the December 8, 1932, issue, the column focused on rabbit with an advertisement for the Bellevue Brown Bunny Rabbitry and its "Carefully Fed Rabbits." An accompanying article included a recipe and extolled the benefits of rabbit meat, reporting that government statistics show its meat containing 83 per cent protein.

Heritage Recipe
Rabbit Fricasee

Soak the rabbit meat in salt water for fifteen minutes after cutting into 8 pieces per rabbit.
Roll each piece in flour or finely crushed cracker crumbs. Saute in half butter-half shortening, add salt and pepper to taste and garlic if desired.
Cover meat and cook, adding a little boiling hot water when needed.

"A wonderful gravy may be made from the fryings."[77]

Under the heading for the Household Column ran this reassuring ditty, probably penned by its poetically-inclined editor:

A little aid,
Just here and there,
Removes from life
Much toil and care.

The Puget Sound Power & Light Company ran ads urging housewives to "be among the thousands of women who are doing better cooking at lower cost. . ." and buy a Westinghouse electric range. One ad included this ditty, and a cat playing a fiddle as an illustration.

The pan and the griddle,
Is often a riddle,
To housewives until they learn ways;
Of electrical cooking,
Without always looking
And drudging long hours thru the days.

A regular column, "From the Kelvin Kitchen" by Joan Adams featured recipes and addressed timely culinary topics; for example, suggestions for entertaining at Thanksgiving and Christmas. She wrote about "Lunch at School," and she once discoursed in length on gingerbread, even venturing into the science of cooking: "Soda is usually used for leavening. . . because gingerbread recipes contain molasses and sour milk, both ingredients of which have the effect of releasing the gas from the soda through acids they contain."[78]

The Porch Party Menu July 12, 1934

The porch party blends picnic informality with the graces of a formal afternoon tea arranged outside for the sake of coolness and to save mother hot hours in the kitchen.[79]

Fruit Refresher Salad
Grapejuice Punch
Cinnamon Thimble Biscuits
Apple Jelly Ice Cream

LeHuquet Extracts: A Cottage Industry

In 1883, Crescent Foods, the Seattle spice firm, began selling vanilla extract door-

to-door. In the 1930's the company gained fame with Mapleine, its answer to maple syrup. By then, the State of Washington was one of the United States' three most important producing areas of peppermint oil.[80] Perhaps influenced by this local industry, LeHuquet began making and selling extracts.

One of his daughters, Ruby, at the age of 86 years described in a 2006 interview her father's extract business: "Eugene LeHuquet came to Washington in 1911 and started a weekly newspaper called *The Lake Washington Reflecter* [sic]. As I recall my mother and father made the extract. I don't remember any other than vanilla, orange and lemon. My father did not sell it locally but worked up a door-to-door business in two areas in Seattle, Capital Hill and West Seattle. I recall that it was popular because the label said "will not bake out". In other words it was a pretty strong extract. The name LeHuquet was on the label. . . ."[81]

LeHuquet Extract Vehicle

Heritage Recipe
Vanilla Extract

Both for medicinal and culinary purposes, people make homemade extracts. Recipes use simple ingredients that need to sit for a period of time, even up to a year, to bring out the flavors.

2 vanilla beans, cut in half lengthwise and chop (1 Tbsp)
1/2 cup brandy
1/4 cup water
Pour brandy and water over vanilla beans in a jar.
Yield: 3/4 cup

Adapted from "Homemade in the Kitchen."[82]

Newspaper Food Columnist Greg Atkinson

Since *The Lake Washington Reflector*, more than a few newspapers have operated in Bellevue. Previous to and throughout the shifting fortunes of local newspapers, the *Seattle Post-Intelligencer* and *The Seattle Times* have served Bellevue. In 1976, *The Seattle Times* East News Bureau opened in Bellevue.[83] Greg Atkinson writes the food column for *The Seattle Times* Sunday "Pacific Magazine" section. His column brings up-to-date Northwest culinary news to Bellevue's readers about local growers, cheese makers and restaurant specialties.

"I started baking these cookies at IslandWood, the environmental learning center on Bainbridge Island. I cut them out with a leaf shaped cookie cutter and marked the cut out cookie dough with the back of a knife to simulate the veins on a leaf. They are beautiful and work well for every cookie occasion from the most casual picnics to the most formal dinners. The large crystals of less-refined sugar never dissolve entirely and lend the cookies an interesting appearance and texture."[84]

Tested
IslandWood Butter Cookies
Greg Atkinson, Food Editor, Seattle Times

1 cup (2 sticks) organic butter
3/4 cup turbinado sugar or "Sugar in the Raw"
2 large egg yolks
1 teaspoon vanilla extract
2 cups plus 2 tablespoons unbleached white flour
1 teaspoon kosher salt
Preheat the oven to 350 degrees F.

Line 2 large baking sheets with baker's parchment or silicone pan liners.
Soften the butter: Cut all the butter into 1-inch chunks. Melt half of it in a saucepan and put the rest in the bowl of an upright mixer. Pour the melted butter over the cold butter and beat until all the butter is smooth and creamy.

Add the sugar and continue beating until the mixture is light and fluffy. Add the egg yolks and the vanilla extract, and beat until the eggs are completely incorporated into the butter and sugar mixture.

Add the flour and salt all at once to the butter mixture and fold gently with a rubber spatula just until the mixture comes together to form soft dough.
Divide the dough into two parts and press each piece of dough into a disk, but don't fuss over it too much or the cookies will be tough. Chill the disks of dough until it is firm enough to roll, about 30 minutes.

Roll the disks of dough, one at a time to 1/8-inch thick and cut with cookie cutters. Bake until golden, about 10 minutes. Cool on pans before moving. The cookies will crisp as they cool.
Yield: 2 dozen large cookies

Food for Gracious Living 1940 to 1970

Restaurants, Bellevue Square Fare, and Supermarkets Celebrating the End of an Era

In 1900, venturesome travelers bumped over curving, unpaved roads around Lake Washington to explore the Eastside. If they crossed Lake Washington from Seattle by boat, they disembarked to find themselves on the edge of dense forest. Steamboats brought passengers from Leschi to docks in Bellevue from 1892 until 1913. In December of 1913, the Leschi, the first ferry boat to carry automobiles across Lake Washington, began its runs from Seattle to the Eastside. It discontinued service to Bellevue in 1921, stopping only at Medina.[1]

The Lacey V. Murrow Bridge opened in 1940 followed by the Albert D. Rossellini Bridge in 1963. Celebrations for the Lake Washington Floating Bridge connecting Seattle and Mercer Island to Bellevue signified the end of Bellevue's early rural years. First came the ground-breaking ceremonies December 18, 1938. "500 jubilant men and women attended a Victory Banquet at the Bellevue Clubhouse to celebrate." On July 2, 1949, the community celebrated at a second banquet to commemorate the removal of tolls on the Lake Washington Floating Bridge. Their removal made travel and commuting less expensive and more convenient. "For the greater development of our state: The removal of tolls on the Lake Washington Bridge eliminates another barrier between the East and West," so read the commemoration. Carl Pefley of the Crabapple Restaurant prepared typically Bellevue fare for the banquet meal.[2]

Bridge Banquet Menu

Whole Spiced Crabapples
Fresh Fruit and Melon Cup Supreme
Hol-Grain Wafers
Dutch Oven Steak, Simmered in Mushroom Sauce
Fresh Green Peas, Buttered and Snow-Flake Potatoes
Walnut Bread and Home-made Crabapple Jelly
Cocoanut Cream Pie
Coffee
Younger's Mints

Town of Gracious Living

After World War II, the center of town life, where people lived, worked, went to school and shopped, began to shift north of Main Street.[3] As Bellevue became more de-centralized, neighborhoods developed. Bellevue began to annex former farmland east of town for new communities of planned tract homes, built as suburban developments convenient to nearby shopping centers and schools. Sherwood Forest and Lake

Hills to the southeast typified this trend.[4] Where strawberry fields and orchards formerly graced Downey Hill, now stood the houses of Vuecrest, the town's first planned neighborhood.[5] Nearby, the opening of Bellevue Square accentuated the shift already begun by Lakeside Center and its supermarket. "Going to the mall" created something new for shoppers, attracted by the one-stop shopping concept and the new restaurants where they could go out to eat.

No longer isolated on farms and with more leisure time, families connected with their neighbors on a daily basis and established broader friendships. Homemakers met for coffee and supervised children's activities. They drove their automobiles to Bellevue Square and to the new private clubs where they met friends for coffee or lunch, and where business associates discussed community matters. Neighbors and friends joined forces to plan for the annual Arts and Crafts Fair and to raise money to build Overlake Hospital. School programs and the Overlake Service League adapted to meet the increasingly diverse needs of children and families.

Before 1940, Bellevue families commuting home on the ferry after work or school from Seattle, dined according to the ferry schedules. Post World War II residents arrived at a more unpredictable hour for their evening meal, driving across the bridge in separate cars at the mercy of the aptly characterized "rush hour." Along with the increasing use of the automobile, drive-in restaurants and fast-food chains became popular. Young people frequented them, meeting friends after school and on weekends for a hamburger or milk shake.

All-American City Palate

In 1955, the National Municipal League and Look magazine designated Bellevue an All-America City: "In recognition of progress in intelligent citizen action."[6] Did Bellevue also have an "All-American" palate? Washington, only a state since 1889, had a population that came predominately from outside the region; they brought recipes with them from wherever they originated. Aside from local berries and tree fruit on menus, a regional cuisine had yet to establish itself. Indeed, during the 1950's and 1960's Bellevue ate from menus that resembled those all over America. At home they ate peanut butter, Ritz crackers, macaroni and cheese, and they did not eat out often. When they did, they knew what menu choices to expect.

*Carl Pefley and
Duncan Hines Award*

Late in the 1950's, customers dined at the Village Inn in the Home Center Building and ordered chicken livers, eastern sugar cured ham steak, fried chicken or Louisiana prawns the latter for $2.20 including potato and salad.[7] Eateries near or in Bellevue

Square included the well-known Crabapple Restaurant and the Kandy Kane Kafe, Kingen's Drive-In, and The Barb in the Ditty Building where prime rib and charcoal broiled steaks or spare ribs were on the menu. They went for breakfast to Hutch's Hut on Main Street and to the Scandia Freeze Shoppe on NE 8th to enjoy "soft freeze in three flavors" and hamburgers.[8]

The Crabapple Restaurant

Carl Pefley's Crabapple Restaurant, Bellevue's earliest "destination" restaurant,

opened in 1946 in Bellevue's first shopping square. Duncan Hines, who crisscrossed the country in search of good quality in restaurant food, recommended the Crabapple dining room and cuisine.

Important for Bellevue's future, Pefley exhibited original paintings by Northwest artists on his restaurant walls, and he also had the idea for the Pacific Northwest Arts and Crafts Fair that became an annual Bellevue event attracting visitors to the town. From 1946 until 1955, community leaders often gathered around the inviting large round table at the Crabapple Restaurant to make plans for the annual fair and for Bellevue Square during its developing years as a commercial center.[10]

Crabapple Restaurant interior circa 1947

Pefley offered sweet pickled crabapples as a starter to the dinner. As noted on the Crabapple menu, Mrs. A.C. Nation and other Bellevue housewives canned two thousand quarts for the restaurant, using locally grown crabapples. Marguerite Groves, Bellevue's first librarian and a friend of Mrs. Nation, left a handwritten recipe for "Spiced Crab Apples," recently discovered in her recipe box. Very likely Mrs. Nation's recipe came from the same source listed on the recipe, from a cookbook entitled How Mama Could Cook.[11]

Heritage Recipe
Spiced Crabapples
Marguerite Groves' Recipe File

3 quarts crabapples
1 quart wine vinegar
2 pounds sugar

1 tablespoon whole allspice
1 tablespoon stick cinnamon
1 tablespoon whole cloves
1 tablespoon black mace

Get apples of equal size. Cut off blossom ends, don't peel. Prick each in its tough skin several times. Mix vinegar, sugar, and spices and boil until syrup is thick enough to coat spoon. Then add the apples, have low heat, simmer until tender. Scoop out fruit, pack in 5 pint jars, sterilized and hot, add boiling syrup to cover, and seal.
Yield: 5 pint jars.

In 1955, Walter Clark added the Bellevue Crabapple to his Seattle chain of restaurants, calling it Clark's Crabapple. The Bellevue menu varied somewhat from the menus at other Clark's restaurants. It featured steaks and broiled seafood cooked on a charcoal broiler and, on Sundays, chicken served "family style" called "Chicken Every Sunday." Clark's decoration of the Crabapple reflected Bellevue's continuing interest in Northwest art. He hung two George Tsutakawa cedar carvings over the fireplace: one of skiers and another showing people with a guitar, "signifying conviviality. . ." Clark's Crabapple operated until 1975.[12]

Kandy Kane Kafe

Carol and Tom Barber owned and operated the Kandy Kane Kafe Coffee Shop in Bellevue Square. A popular coffee stop for Bellevue merchants and residents from 1950 until 1965, it served as the meeting place for founders of Bellevue's new hospital. Carol Barber had a special talent for fundraising and put on vaudeville shows to benefit the new facility. She often appeared at the old Palomar Theater. She loved to perform "Won't You Come Home, Bill Bailey," singing and doing a soft shoe dance. In 1965, the Barbers became Managers-Caretakers of the Meydenbauer Bay Yacht Club.[14]

Kandy Kane Kafe, Carol Barber and Bellevue Citizens, circa 1960

Pancake Corral

In 1958, Bill Chace opened the Pancake Corral on Lake Washington Boulevard SE, south of downtown Bellevue, after operating several Coffee Corrals in Seattle. Chace claimed that if twenty-five percent of his customers came back, he never needed to advertise. "Customers come, then they come with their kids, and then their kids start coming."

Chace's
PANCAKE CORRAL
Family Owned and Operated
Since 1958

"Pancake Day Proceeds to Benefit Hospital" reads the February 26, 1959, *Bellevue American* headline. Designated as "Hospital Pancake Day" all proceeds that day from pancake sales at the Pancake Corral, except for waitresses' salaries, were donated to the building fund for Bellevue's new hospital. Waitresses also donated their tips.[15] Overlake blueberry pancakes with hot compote, strawberry waffles with fresh strawberries and ice cream, chocolate waffles with ice cream and sauce, Alaska sourdough flapjacks as well as traditional pancakes and waffles brought very willing contributors to the hospital benefit at the Pancake Corral.

Bill Chace died in 2001, but very little else has changed at the Pancake Corral since opening forty-eight years ago. The family still operates the business, preserving it as an "old fashioned place." Waitresses write up the orders and add up the bills. Nothing is pre-cooked, and good quality ingredients go into their "cooked-to-order" menu items.[16]

Arthur's Bakery

Other bakeshops came and went, but Arthur Wilk with his popular cakes and pastries created a Bellevue institution that endured thirty-eight years, from 1956 to 1994. How many of Arthur's birthday cakes and desserts adorned Bellevue's tables, bringing friends, families and community leaders together? That

Elaine Wilk Decorates Bellevue Square Celebration Cake 1981

number includes the blueberry pies for the blueberry festivals, from 1957 to 1959, and according to the Wilks, the "biggest cake ever baked in Bellevue" for the 1981 Grand Opening of the renovated Bellevue Square.

Arthur Wilk opened Arthur's Bakery in Bellevue in 1956, and his was no ordinary bakery shop. His wife, Elaine, a fine artist, created beautifully decorated cakes, and Arthur baked quality breads, black and light rye, wheat and egg sesame, only in twenty-pound batches so they would sell out while still fresh. In the 1950's, customers paid 27 cents for a small loaf of bread and 89 cents for a lemon pie. Steve and Kasia Wilk, born into the bakery business, also contributed to Arthur's success. The Wilk's daughter, Kasia, became head cake decorator and later shop manager. According to Steve, the bakery was "the center of our earth, our identity, our life style. Saturday, we all went to the bakery, and when I was tall enough, my dad would let me help make the doughnuts. Then in the afternoon my sister, Kasia, and I would go to the mall to spend our dollar allowance. It cost 25 cents to go to the movie theatre."

The bakery regularly donated baked foods, they called it the "nun run," to the Sacred Heart Convent, located on the site of the present-day Clyde Hill church. In 1964, the Wilks built their own baker-designed building where customers could watch the baking process. The Wilks baked for Bellevue's taste and created a loyal clientele, happy memories and enduring relationships.[17]

Bellevue Square

In the 1940's, after the opening of the first bridge to the Eastside from Seattle, Miller Freeman and his son, Kemper Freeman, Sr. envisioned the commercial development of a Bellevue shopping center. After visiting other projects around the country, Kemper Freeman, Sr. favored a one-stop shopping center concept. When Bellevue Square opened in 1946, it offered sixteen stores including Frederick & Nelson, the Bel-Vue Theatre, Petram's Variety Store, Sparling's Hardware, the Food Center, Gordon Baker's Barber Shop and the Crabapple Restaurant.[18]

When Bellevue incorporated in 1953 as a third class city it officially encompassed five square miles and counted 5,940 citizens. Kemper Freeman, Jr continues the family business enterprises in Bellevue. His wife, Betty, says although the Freeman family has participated in Bellevue's development, that no one could have anticipated Bellevue would evolve the way it has. "When we started out it was just a small charming little town; now, it's a city."[19]

Freeman Family Caroling Party

In 1958, Kemper Freeman, Sr. made application for Bellevue's first radio station with his initials as its call letters, KFKF. The radio station acquired a vintage 1921 fire engine, and the senior Kemper Freeman enjoyed driving it around for promotional events. In the late 1960's, Betty and Kemper Freeman, Jr. invited friends to go Christmas caroling around town in the fire truck. Everyone dressed up warmly in their ski clothes to ride in its open carriage for the caroling, and after an evening of song returned to the

Freeman Fire Engine Caroling Party circa 1960

Freemans for a potluck dinner. The event became a tradition for the Freemans and their friends. Although the Freemans eventually gave up caroling, for some years the fire engine brought Santa to the Square on the day after Thanksgiving as a part of the Children's Christmas Parade.[20]

Frederick & Nelson's Frango Mints

In 1946, Frederick & Nelson became the flagship store for the newly opened Bellevue Square. Founded in 1918, Frederick & Nelson featured a candy counter and tea

room in their stores and had their own kitchens. Anyone who grew up in Bellevue and Seattle during this era remembers Frederick & Nelson tea rooms as the place to go for lunch or tea and holiday brunches. Among other menu items, patrons especially enjoyed the bread, hand-made in the tea room kitchens, and the Olympic berry sherbet, from a recipe using local berries. Frederick & Nelson developed one especially popular recipe, Frango ice cream, and not long afterward, a candy they called Frango mints.[21]

Bellevue Frederick & Nelson Tea Room

The candy became intertwined with the store's identity, and with the companies that later acquired Frederick & Nelson. Marshall Fields bought out Frederick & Nelson in 1929, including the right to distribute its unique cube-shaped candies in their recognizable mint green round boxes. In the beginning, Frederick & Nelson made the original recipe in their own Seattle kitchens. Then, a company in Kent, Frederick's Fine Chocolates, produced the candies; later Seattle Gourmet Foods made them. Frango mints gained national fame over the years, and even became the focus of litigation when the Frederick & Nelson bankruptcy forced the store to close its doors in 1992. The rival Seattle department store, the Bon Marché, obtained the right to use the name and make Frango's. Macy's, owner since 2005 of both the Bon Marché and Marshall Fields, currently sells the famous candies.[22]

Frango's Box circa 1950

*Bellevue Frederick & Nelson Candy Counter
circa 1950*

The complicated history of Frango's and the protracted struggle for the right to make them precludes obtaining the secret recipe. The ingredients include chocolate, triple-distilled oil from Oregon peppermint and 40 percent butter.[23] The following recipe includes Frango's as an ingredient.

Tested
Frango's Cookies
Toni Keene, Gourmet Chef & Food Specialist[24]
A delicious variation, this chocolate chip recipe produces a rich, chewy-crisp cookie.

1 1/4 cups flour
1/2 teaspoon baking soda
1/2 teaspoon salt (optional)
1/2 cup granulated sugar
1/4 cup brown sugar, packed
1/2 cup shortening
1 egg
1 teaspoon vanilla
1 box Frango's (any flavor) cut into 4 or 5 pieces each

Preheat oven to 350 degrees F. With mixer, cream together sugars and shortening till smooth and creamy. Add egg, vanilla, baking soda, salt, and flour, mixing well. By hand, stir in Frango candy pieces.
Drop teaspoon-size balls on non-stick or parchment-lined cookie sheet.
Bake 8 to 10 minutes.
Yield: 45 cookies.

Nordstrom's Nordy Bar

In 1958, Nordstrom opened a shoe store in Bellevue Square. In 1965, the store expanded to include fashion. In 1967, the Nordstrom Company built the Bellevue Nordstrom Store, 77,000 square feet, as one of the anchors of Bellevue Square. They moved to the present-day location in 1982.

Nordstrom founded its Restaurant Division in 1980 with the purchase of Ryan's Express and introduced Nordy bars around 1985. The chocolate-butterscotch treat they called a Nordy bar and a 25 cent cup of coffee established many a loyal customer for Nordstrom. Serving on-site reasonably priced food in the Bellevue store's café fit naturally into the Nordstrom philosophy of giving service to customers. Seattle's coffee revolution brought coffee bars to the Bellevue store. In 1994, they opened an Espresso Bar, for "on-the-go" shoppers, at the west entrance. From 1980 to 1999, Nordstrom cardholders could buy a cup of coffee for 25 cents.[25]

Dorothy Johnson Scott had the distinction of being the first woman hired to work at the Seattle Nordstrom. She worked there from 1925 until she retired in 1939. Her daughter, Marilyn Scott Goesling became an employee from 1963 to 1968; in the 1980's an employee friend gave her the recipe for the Nordy bar.[26]

Tested
Nordy Bars
Marilyn Goesling

This rich, caramel-chocolate bar can be served as a cookie or a dessert with whipped cream.

1/2 cup butter
1-12 ounce package butterscotch chips
1/2 cup brown sugar
2 eggs
1 1/2 cups flour
2 teaspoons baking powder
1/2 teaspoon salt
2 teaspoons vanilla
1-12 ounce package chocolate chips
2 cups miniature marshmallows
1 cup chopped nuts

Preheat oven 350 degrees F.
Melt butter. Stir in butterscotch chips and brown sugar until melted. Remove from heat. Add eggs, flour, baking powder and salt, mixing thoroughly. Cool and add vanilla. Mix in chocolate chips, marshmallows and chopped nuts. Spread in a greased 9" by 13" pan.
Bake 25 minutes. Cool and cut into squares.
Yield: 36 bars

Supermarket Shopping

Before World War II, people in Bellevue shopped in small grocery stores, including McGauvran's, Henry Streams' and Bill Crooker's.[27]   Typically, a clerk waited on each customer, and there was little variety available. Customers purchased canned

Lakeside Supermarket circa 1944

goods, flour, sugar, coffee and other non-perishable items. They went to Seattle for fresh fruits and vegetables. Small groceries also served as gathering places. Nat Green remembers men meeting at Crooker's grocery where they sat on potato sacks in the back room to catch up on the town's news.[28]

In 1916, Piggly Wiggly opened the first supermarket in the United States, allowing customers to serve themselves and stocking the shelves with several brands of a product.[29] Bellevue waited over 13 years to acquire its first supermarket. James Ditty purchased land on the southeast corner of Bellevue Way and NE 8th. He developed the Lakeside Center, and opened Bellevue's first supermarket called the Lakeside Supermarket.[30]

Quality Food Centers

Developers in 1955 built a new subdivision southeast of Bellevue planned for 4,000 homes and a shopping center. Modeled after a planned community in Levittown, New York, it became known as Lake Hills. In 1956, Jack Crocco opened the first Quality Food Center store, the beginning of the QFC chain, in the Lake Hills Shopping Center. He envisioned a store where customers found both quality food and service. This first store became the prototype. "The 13,000 square foot 'supermarket' had gleaming floors, beautiful produce, a convenient layout, and exceptionally courteous employees. Each QFC customer was greeted with a smile. Energetic 'box boys' carried shopping bags to each customer's car. Jack learned his customers' names and did everything he could to make grocery shopping a pleasant experience at the Lake Hills QFC. He taught his 'troops' to do the same and the reputation of QFC grew. Jack soon had three stores."[31]

The Bellevue Village QFC had its grand opening in 1967 at 100th Avenue NE and NE 8th, the site of the historic Baker House. Jim Wire, manager of the Bellevue QFC since 1982, points proudly to the innovations piloted by the store. In the mid-1980's, the Bellevue store was the first to incorporate a coffee shop, Veneto's. It also offered the first in-store seafood counter and prime beef. QFC contributes to the communities it serves. The Bellevue store provides products and gift certificates to the Bellevue Boys and Girls Club, to schools and for the Clyde Hill Days Event. Since 2003, the Bellevue QFC has donated all the strawberries for Bellevue's Strawberry Festival.[32]

Gatherings around the Table for the Arts and a Hospital

Arts and Crafts Fair

In the 1930's and 1940's, the Strawberry Festival brought together the Bellevue community to celebrate its bountiful strawberry crops, but World War II forced its cancellation. Bellevue turned from agriculture to business and created a new community focus, the Pacific Northwest Arts and Crafts Fair, founded in 1947. The first fair opened in the original unenclosed Bellevue Square where

Pacific Northwest Arts and Crafts Fair, circa 1950

artists and crafts makers set up display tables and exhibits under the eaves and along the sidewalks. Thirty thousand attended the first fair in Bellevue, then only a town of less than five thousand residents.[33] Visitors viewed exhibits of pottery, quilts, wooden toys, paintings, glass and wearable art. Over the years, a number of artists who showed at the fair later became highly acclaimed. To name only a few, they included Doris Chase, Dale Chihuly, Ron Ho, Ted Rand, and George Tsutakawa.[34] Food became an integral part of the fairs.

Blueberry Festival at the Fair

In 1951, Bellevue's blueberries came to the fair, inaugurating a decade of Blueberry Festival activities concurrent with the art fair. The Bellevue Chamber of Commerce constructed two booths and featured blueberry pie, tarts and muffins sold by the piece with ice cream and coffee. Volunteers from the Women's Society of the Community First Congregational Church baked and served the fresh pies and muffins. Many others contributed, including the Pacific

*Overlake Blueberry Label
circa 1947*

*Blueberry Festival:
"Princess and blueberries..."
circa 1957*

Northwest Blueberry Growers' Association which furnished 750 pounds of berries; Fisher Flouring Mills, all the flour; Pacific Fruit & Produce, sugar; Proctor & Gamble, Crisco; and Happy Valley Farms, cream and ice cream equipment. From 1957 to 1959, Arthur's Bakery purchased berries from the Overlake Blueberry Farm and baked all the pies sold at Bellevue's Blueberry Festival.[35]

*Tested
Arthur's Blueberry Festival Pie*

The crust browns nicely. Add additional cinnamon for a more flavorful pie and, especially when using frozen berries, add additional flour to thicken the filling. Delicious with whipped or ice cream.

*Crust
2 cups all-purpose flour
1 teaspoon salt
2/3 cup cold shortening
1/4 cup cold water*

*Directions
Place flour and salt in bowl.
Cut shortening into flour.*

Sprinkle with one tablespoon of water at a time.
Mix lightly with fork until all flour is moistened.
Gather half of dough into a ball and roll out to line a 9 inch pie pan.
Roll out remainder for top pie crust.

Blueberry Filling
1 to 1 1/2 cups granulated sugar
1/3 cups all purpose flour
1/2 teaspoon cinnamon
4 to 4 1/2 cups blueberries (fresh or frozen)
1 1/2 tablespoons butter

Preheat oven to 425 degrees F.
Combine flour, sugar and cinnamon. Stir dry ingredients lightly through the blueberries
Pour into pie plan lined with the pie dough. Dot with butter. Cover with top crust, seal edges and slit top. Bake 35 to 45 minutes in a preheated oven.
Yield: 1 9-inch pie

Fair Food Charities

The tradition of selling food for charitable causes probably began with the Medina-Evergreen Circle of the Overlake Service League. In 1950, its volunteers converted their Service League store into a tea shop, offering "rest and light refreshment" to weary art patrons.[36]

In the 1960's, art guilds formed to raise money to support the fair and build a museum. Yvonne Miller, fair coordinator three times and founding member of the Miller Freeman Guild, remembers that in

Bellevue Arts Museum
Arts and Crafts Fair, 2006

the 1970's, the guilds sponsored a salmon barbecue held in a replica of a longhouse erected outside of the Bon Marché. Throughout the Arts and Crafts Fair, they grilled the salmon and served it with coleslaw and bread for $1.50.[37]

Many of the charitable food booths have become an annual tradition. Bellevue Rotary members push refrigerated carts on wheels and sell ice cream bars, Kiwanis Club members cook spit-barbecued hot beef for their famous sandwiches, the Greater Bellevue Lions Club grills hot dogs, and sales of popping Kettle Korn benefit Elder Adult Day Services.[38]

Patrons Parties

After the success of the first fair in 1947, the Pacific Northwest Arts & Crafts Association organized to plan future fairs and, eventually, to open an art museum. In 1953,

Bellevue's first Arts and Crafts Fair Patrons Party gave interested buyers an opportunity to meet the prize-winning artists and purchase their art before the opening day of the fair. In the early decades these were strictly mixed-drink cocktail events often held on the lawns of beautiful west Bellevue private homes where easels displayed the art for viewing.[39] In the 1990's, Bellevue Botanical Gardens hosted the parties. By then, the parties were more elaborate. Art patrons viewed the art while sipping a glass of wine and enjoying a creative buffet of appetizers that included canapés, cheeses and chocolate-dipped strawberries piled high and displayed on trays.

In 2006, the Patrons Party supporters celebrated sixty years of fair history, holding the event in the Bellevue Arts Museum, its new building inaugurated in 2000. The museum recently re-opened after a closure of more than a year due to financial challenges. Museum members and community leaders came to show their support and enthusiasm for the museum, for its new director, Michael Monroe, and the Board. They celebrated at a stand-up buffet, catered by the new Lincoln Square McCormick and Schmicks restaurant. Two long serving tables displayed trays of hot, delicately moist salmon, chicken satay, shrimp cocktail, mussels on the shell with salmon roe, cheeses, breads, pork slices, tomato and mozzarella on skewers, and thinly sliced melons. Dessert tables featured chocolate cookie balls and miniature currant and cream tarts. They also enjoyed Washington wines and a special pomegranate cocktail. A live auction of ten objets d'art raised $51,600. Other gifts totaled an additional $30,000 targeted for the museum's educational fund.[40]

"It was unlike any others we've attended. Since it was the 60th [year for the fair], several artists had been asked to create something that had '60' imbedded in them in some way. . . Food was excellent. . .very festive all the way around," said Arlene Alton museum docent, about the 2006 Patrons Party.[41]

Art Guild Cookbooks

To raise funds for the fair and development of an art museum in the 1960's, the Pacific Northwest Arts & Crafts Association organized guilds whose members compiled and sold cookbooks to benefit the fair and a future museum. Some served their recipes at luncheon meetings.[42]

Heritage
Watercress Cheese Canapés
Lynn (Lin) Clark Salisbury "The See Cookbook" Miller Freeman Guild

Heat cheese and only slightly wilt the watercress for best flavor.
24 1/2-inch rounds white bread
4 cups watercress - trimmed of stems, loosely packed
2 tablespoons butter
1/3 pound Port Salut cheese, diced
Toast the bread on both sides and keep warm

In a saucepan, melt butter. Add finely diced cheese and heat, stirring until melted.
Off of heat stir in watercress. Mound onto the toast rounds and serve immediately
Yield: 24

Overlake Hospital
Roasted Turkeys Arrive by Ambulance

In 1940, the newly opened Lake Washington Floating Bridge enabled more young families to locate in Bellevue. A house on Clyde Hill cost $5000, while a comparable home in Seattle sold for $7000. However, Bellevue had no hospital for medical emergencies. When Dr. James McGrath moved to Bellevue early in the 1950's, becoming the town's first full-time pediatrician, he made house calls. He was on-call 24 hours a day, seven days a week. For a number of years, his wife Charlotte not only raised their five children, but also acted as his answering service. After Overlake Hospital's opening, he served as its first chief of pediatrics and as hospital chief of staff. McGrath retired in 1989.[43]

By 1953, citizens had formed the Overlake Memorial Hospital Association to raise money for a hospital in Bellevue. Lorraine Weltzien and Anna Seeger recruited neighbors to form the first hospital auxiliary, the Fabiola Auxiliary. When the hospital finally became a reality October 16, 1960, the auxiliaries organized a costume party, a very popular 1960's theme to celebrate the Grand Opening. Volunteers decorated the new hospital lobby and set it up for dinner. When guests were seated, ambulances dramatically delivered platters of whole roasted turkeys and all the trimmings stacked on hospital gurneys; bedpans served as ashtrays! Those attending got into the spirit by coming in costume. Lorraine Weltzien remembers Dr. Chuck and Pat Griffith, posing as "Upper GI" and "Lower GI," dressed in army fatigues with the appropriate x-rays hanging around their necks.[44]

More recently, the Overlake Auxiliaries raised $1.3 million at the 2006 Bandage Ball held at the Meydenbauer Center, much of it through auction purchases of "one-of-a-kind experiences," often a culinary one. Donors purchased a cocktail party at Seattle artist Steve Jensen's Capitol Hill studio, a wine-tasting party at Woodinville Cellars, a dinner with Husky Men's Basketball Coach Lorenzo Romar and his wife, a Chef's Table dinner at the Westin Bellevue, a paella party on Lake Sammamish, dinner at the Chateau Ste. Michelle winery, and a Puerto Rican-style pig roast at the home of Mariner legend Edgar Martinez and his wife Holli. With the proceeds from these and other auction items in addition to an anonymous $300,000 gift, the hospital purchased a CT system for the hospital's emergency department.[45]

Overlake Hospital Auxiliary Cookbooks

Eleanor Roosevelt visited the Northwest after her daughter, Anna, married John Boettiger, who published the *Seattle Post-Intelligencer* from 1936 to 1943. The Boettigers lived on Mercer Island and had close friends in Bellevue where they often visited.

Overlake Hospital auxiliaries printed cookbooks to benefit hospital projects. Appearing in the Spiritwood Auxiliary's *Festive Feeds Cookbook*, Eleanor Roosevelt's recipe typifies a more frugal approach to cooking, probably an influence of the Depression and the war years.[46]

She described it simply:

Heritage Recipe
Eleanor Roosevelt's Huckleberry Pudding

Layer bread slices and cover with cooked and sweetened huckleberries.
Chill and serve with whipped cream.

Hospital Auxiliary Cookie Exchange Parties

The cookie exchange party became popular during the middle years of the twentieth century when communities were developing across America. These gatherings gave new neighbors an opportunity to become acquainted and volunteers in organizations an occasion for an informal meeting. Typically, each participant brought five dozen of a favorite recipe to exchange and another dozen to share at the party. Everyone went home with a variety of cookies to use for entertaining throughout the holiday season.[47]

The Elizabeth Blackwell Auxiliary holiday cookie exchange parties were held at Jane Wood's home. These crunchy, buttery balls melt in the mouth. With slight variations in ingredients, they appear regularly on holiday cookie trays, also called Mexican wedding cakes, Russian tea cakes, or Pecan sandies.

Tested
Danish Butter Balls
Suzanne Hutchinson

1 cup butter
1/4 cup sugar
2 teaspoons vanilla
1/2 teaspoon salt
2 cups flour
1 cup ground almonds
1 cup ground pecans
1/8 teaspoon mace

Preheat oven to 300 degrees F. Cream butter, sugar, vanilla and salt.
Mix the mace with the flour and stir into the creamed mixture. Add nuts.
Cover and chill the dough for a few hours or overnight.
Put a small amount of the mixture into your hands and shape into a ball a little smaller than a walnut.
Bake for 30 minutes.

When cool, roll balls in confectioner's sugar twice. (can put several balls into a paper bag with sifted sugar and shake to cover.)
Yield: 4 dozen.

Home Cooking and Club Food Events

Norwood Village: "Village Vittles"

Bellevue Boys Club Teen Canteen 1955

Many new families arriving in Bellevue in the 1950's settled in Bellevue's new communities of planned homes. Norwood Village became a prototype for new communities of this era. It came into being when a group of 100 veterans of World War II organized the Veterans Mutual Building Association and, for $875, purchased 30 acres south and east of Bellevue's downtown. They hired architects who designed homes for young families eager to establish themselves and create traditions. They wanted space to entertain their families and new friends. A basic 890 square foot house cost $10,500 and featured a modern kitchen, a combination dining and living room and an outdoor terrace.[48]

In the 1950's, many women did not work outside the home, at least during the years they were raising their families. As a result, homemakers dedicated more time to cooking for family, friends and for good causes. Norwood Village wives compiled a recipe book entitled, *"Village Vittles."*[49]

Dedication

We, the Norwood Wives,
Who spend our lives
And all of our days
To please those gourmets-
Our Husbands.
So dedicate this collection
Of culinary perfection to those men so arresting
Who've done all the testing-
Our Husbands.
With special salute
To gentlemen astute
Who prove in this book
Husbands also can cook.

Village Vittles Cookbook circa 1950

Most of the recipes have little connection to Northwest foods because many Norwood Village and Bellevue residents were recent "transplants," more often than not from other sections of the country. Quite a few recipes in the book utilized commercial products popular at the time. Canned soups appear in recipes for tuna casserole, hamburger pie and tomato soup cake. A date and nut cake calls for one cup of mayonnaise; ranger cookies, for Rice Krispies or Corn Flakes. A section entitled "Puddings" includes a recipe for Lemon Grapenuts Pudding. Ozark Bakeless Pudding consisted of alternating layers of crushed graham crackers and canned crushed pineapple; Jello dessert, of dissolved lime jello, cream cheese and mayonnaise. The book includes a recipe for making five pounds of fruit cake and seasonal menus for children.

Spring Menu "Little Folk Lawn Party- for 3 to 6-year-olds

"Some sunny Spring afternoon invite a few of your three-year-old's chums to bring their favorite Toy's [sic] and play on your lawn. Ask the mothers to come, too. This menu will please all."

Lawn Party Menu

Finger Vegetables
Tiny Tea Sandwiches
Ice Cream Flower Pots*
Pink Lemonade

*Ice Cream Flower Pots. Remove the covers from ice cream cups as you take them from the refrigerator. Place on individual plates and stick a lollipop in the center of each "flower pot." Insert two thin peppermint poles of different heights at angles to the lollipop and top each with a colored candy circle. Make pink lemonade by adding cranberry juice or food coloring.[50]

The New Western Homemaker

Publications for homemakers began to appear on newsstands and offered guidelines for living in the new suburbs springing up across America. One such magazine, *Living for Young Homemakers*, featured Norwood Village in its September 1952 issue. In addition to house plans, it included one photo of Norwood Village mothers teaching their little daughters to cook in a model kitchen.[51]

Tillers and Golf Clubs in Hand, Club Members Support Charity
Meydenbauer Bay Yacht Club and Overlake Golf & Country Club

Before World War II, the Bellevue and Highland Community Clubs offered a meeting place where Bellevue's small town population celebrated and held community meetings. In the 1950's, private clubs provided new venues for events that benefited the community.

Bellevue's lake front location attracted boating enthusiasts who organized the Meydenbauer Bay Yacht Club, incorporating in 1946. Bill Lagen, long time Bel-

levue resident and former city councilman, was the
grandson of William Schupp, the owner and President of the American Pacific Whaling Company,
headquartered on Meydenbauer Bay. In 1933, Mr.
Schupp purchased the adjoining vacated Wildwood
Park Dance Hall to build his future private resi-
dence overlooking the bay. The Meydenbauer Bay
Yacht Club purchased the property from the Lagen
Family. In 1953, six years after incorporation, the
celebration party for the club's opening became its
first event.

Meydenbauer Bay Yacht Club

In 1951, women of the club organized to support local philanthropies and programs
for local nursing homes. The club continues to sponsor several sail and power regat-
tas, as well as the Youth Sailing Program that provides sailing lessons to all interested
young people of the area. Members participate in community activities such as the
Meydenbauer Bay Christmas Ship program with the City of Bellevue Parks and Recreation Department, the Special People's Cruise, and the Opening Day Boat Parade.[52]

Overlake Golf & Country Club

The Overlake Golf & Country Club, located off 84th Avenue NE in Medina, created a
new social venue when, in 1953, a group of members leased the property from Norton Clapp
and reopened a 1927 club formerly on the site. Currently 400 members and their guests
gather at the club for events, often for private parties and wedding receptions. Mothers'
Day and Santa brunches and special dinners are featured events.

Since 1995, The Overlake Golf & Country Club's Women's Golf Division annually organizes the "Nine of Hearts" tournament and
auction to raise funds, often as much as $20,000, for
good causes. In 1998 and 1999, they donated to Cancer Link. Member Jan Conrad founded Cancer Link
after her daughter, Michelle, only 19 years old and
diagnosed with a rare lymphoma, had difficulty finding a support group. Eventually, Overlake Hospital
adopted the Cancer Link program for its patients.[53]
More recently the "Nine of Hearts" efforts benefited

Overlake Golf & Country Club
Benefit Dessert

the Pasado Safe Haven organization. The club serves as the site of an annual auction
for the Ronald MacDonald House at the Children's Orthopedic Hospital. Employees
donate their time and the club donates the food at cost for the event as well as the
opportunity for children involved in the Ronald MacDonald program to ride on the
Christmas boats. In 2007, the Eighteen-Holers will sponsor "First Tee", a national
event , that gives underprivileged children the opportunity to play golf.[54]

September 7, 2006 Nine of Hearts Benefit Menu

Morning Refreshments

Fresh Fruit, Coffee, Tea, Juice and Heart-shaped Mini Scones
Luncheon
Avocado Soup with Heart-shaped Crouton
Fresh Strawberry Spinach Salad & Poppy Seed Dressing,
Puff Pastry Heart with Tomato & Gorgonzola
Dessert
Assorted Mini Cupcakes

Schools as Culinary Connections

Hot Lunch Program History

At the height of the Depression, an unusual volunteer and institutional effort made hot lunches available to Bellevue School children. Borghild Ringdall and her husband ran a berry farm during the Depression; berries they couldn't sell, they distributed to the welfare lines in Seattle. Ringdall, who served on Bellevue school boards in the 1930's, made it her mission to organize a centralized hot lunch program for the Bellevue School District, beginning in 1936 in the Highland School. In 1941, the school program allowed children to buy a hot lunch for 5 cents a day or $1.00 a month. Ringdall later became head cook for the high school.[55]

Belle-View Brand Vegetable Label circa 1940

In the program's early years, the Bellevue Vegetable Growers Association donated vegetables; the summer of 1941 they donated 240 pounds of peas to support the hot lunch program. Teachers and parents canned them. The newspaper announced, "Soup! Soup! Soup!. . . we have sixty-eight gallons of vegetable soup so our first graders will have some hot lunches."[56]

In the twenty-first century, the community recognizes that some Bellevue school children come from less fortunate families. In fact, every school probably has a few children who need assistance. The school district provides free and reduced lunches for children in need. A school lunch costs $2.25; the reduced rate is 40 cents. For the district, 12.8 percent of lunches are free; 4.6 per cent, reduced. A few schools may have almost 50 percent of their children receiving free lunches. In other schools, only one or two percent of children need the program.[57]

Community Support for Lunch Programs

Penny O'Byrne, a member since the 1970's, appreciates the value of partnerships and the flexibility of Overlake Service League programs. "When a program didn't work anymore, we were able to change." In one instance, they identified the need to provide breakfast and lunch during Bellevue public school vacation breaks for Eastside children needing free or reduced-cost lunches.[58] Trish Carpenter heads a committee that annually organizes events to fund the Bellevue School Breaktime - Mealtime program. For example, they raised $79,000 at a wine event held October 21, 2004, at the Dale Chihuly Boat House in Seattle.

For the spring break 2005 project, Nancy Quinn coordinated packing 797 boxes to feed 1,178 children; a partner, Top Foods at Crossroads, supplied basic provisions, food vouchers and suggested menus. The Bellevue School District assists the Overlake Service League with the program. The district sends letters and applications to families in need and makes the school warehouse and trucks available for the breakfast and lunch food box deliveries to schools. Hopelink is another agency that provides extra food for families with school-age children. During the summer months, they offer their "End Summer Hunger" program with food available at the Food Bank.[59]

Antique Lunch Box circa 1920

School Lunch Menu

In the late 1950's, until she retired in 1982, Mitzie Hashiguchi worked as Assistant Supervisor of Elementary School lunches. Mitzie remembers some of the dishes served in those early years: chicken pot pie, macaroni and cheese, tuna casserole, bread pudding, milk and cookies. Two women bakers, Norwegians Selma Erickson and Thelma Larsen, baked all the bread.

With the expansion of the school district and the addition of more schools, the food service gradually became less centralized and more automated. Government regulations affected the menus, as did changing demographics. They began serving pizza and burritos and purchasing bread and pastries, Hostess Twinkies in the early years. In the 1970's, a school lunch cost 35 cents, and hot dogs were second only to hamburgers in popularity. They also served fresh vegetables; the children preferred eating the dessert applesauce on their hotdogs. Vending machines with soft drinks became commonplace in schools. In response to new families moving to Bellevue from all over the world to work in new Eastside technology companies, Bellevue schools offered more diverse lunch and food choices, including Stevenson Elementary's Wednesday Japanese lunch.[60]

International Culinary Influences

Learning French at the Table

Irene Legatte recalls that, between her first experience in 1957 teaching French in the Bellevue School District, and when she returned in 1968, there had been notable changes in her absence. "There was heightened interest in foreign languages and the District provided paid time for teachers to work on curriculum development. I was fortunate to be involved in a French Exchange initiated by Patricia McLean. By this time there was also more ethnic diversity, and Japanese and Chinese were added to the French, German and Spanish programs.

Students always responded to 'cultural events' which involved learning vocabulary related to recipes they were preparing for a dinner at a student's or teacher's home. Students found it less intimidating to master vocabulary related to meals, and they conversed more comfortably with each other. They also delighted in being able to pronounce and translate menu items for family and friends. They became well-acquainted with coq au vin, mousse au chocolat, boeuf bourgignon, etc."[61] Irene's daughter, Donna, attended Jim Hanna's French class dinners; the class prepared the following recipe, without the alcohol.

Tested
Fraises Romanoff
Strawberries Romanoff

It is the orange flavor that makes these strawberries "Romanoff." For use in the schools, eliminate the alcohol in this recipe,

> *1 quart ripe strawberries*
> *1/2 cup strained fresh orange juice*
> *1/2 cup Grand Marnier, Curacao or Cointreau (optional)*
> *1 cup heavy cream, chilled*
> *2 tablespoons confectioner's sugar, sifted*
> *1/2 teaspoon vanilla extract*
> *Crystallized violets (optional)*

Pick over the berries carefully, discarding any that are bruised. Wash the berries quickly under cold water, pat them gently dry with paper towels and remove their stems and hulls. Place the berries in a deep bowl and pour the liqueur and orange juice over them. Cover the bowl and refrigerate the berries for at least 3 hours, turning them gently from time to time.

Just before serving, whip the cream in a large chilled bowl with a wire whisk or a rotary or electric beater. When the cream begins to thicken, add the sugar and vanilla. Continue to beat until the cream forms "unwavering" peaks on beater when it is lifted from the bowl.

Transfer the strawberries and all their juices to a serving bowl. Using a pastry bag with a decorative tip, pipe the cream over the berries or ladle the cream over the berries. Decorate with the crystallized violets.
Yield: 4 to 6 servings

International Influences at Bellevue Community College

Just as college educates and influences students, students, in turn, have an impact on the community. Many Bellevue Community College students live in Bellevue, and, sometimes, remain there after graduation. Their cultural and culinary traditions create a demand for ethnic stores and restaurants. In 1971, five years after Bellevue Community College opened, Kristi Weir took a part-time position in Economics and remained at BCC until retiring in the year 2000. Kristi recalls significant changes during her years at the college. "World events - including economic conditions - changed the demographics of my classes. It started with a wave of Vietnam vets, then returning women, Iranian students, other Middle Eastern students, various Asian contingents - Hong Kong Chinese, Vietnamese and Cambodian refugees, mainland Chinese, and Indonesians - and finally many Eastern Europeans."[62]

Toy's Café: "Growing Up Eating Toy's"

Since the late 1950's, under a succession of owners, Toy's Café has operated in Bellevue as one of its longest continuously operating establishments. Toy's opened when ethnic food still seemed unusual in Bellevue. Its frame building at the intersection of 103rd Avenue NE and Main Street dates from 1918; photos and maps show it was used at one time as a bus station. Charles H. Younger, creator of specialty  candies, opened a café in what had served previously as the Bellevue Bus Terminal Waiting Room. According to a 1926 newspaper report, he catered to candy connoisseurs, soda fountain fans and those waiting for the bus. He also served light lunches and confections. The building also became the location for Anna and Ida's Lakeside Café and Green's Café.[63]

Most Bellevue residents recognized Toy's Café with its awning and modest storefront. Its front window featured advertising for Mandarin and Szechwan cuisine in English and Chinese characters alongside eighteen illustrated platters. Inside, behind the counter hung a vintage Arden Milk clock, a tribute to Arden Farms, a dairy that served Seattle from the 1930's to 1976.[64]

Its unassuming interior bustles with activity. Since 2000, it has been under the diligent attention of owners, Irene and Lai Yin Hon. Customers arrive at all hours throughout the day to enjoy the House Special Soup, Moo Shu Pork, lots of hot tea and rice, as well as other specialties. One visitor remarked, "People hang out at Toy's like they do at Starbuck's."

Anna Hon, their daughter, says that because of the restaurant's long history, they have customers who "grew up eating Toy's" and have moved away but come back to visit. They tell stories of how they came to Toy's for their birthday, or couples will tell of their first date at the restaurant. They may request "Chow Yuk" any stir-fry with added almonds. The dish is not on the Hon's menu, but they are happy to make it, since it reminds the customers of the earlier days of the café.[65]

In September, 2006, when developers purchased the original historic site, the Hons moved Toy's to Main Street at 107th Avenue NE. They took with them the Arden Milk clock and their recipes, preserving Bellevue's culinary history and its Chinese connection. The Chinese restaurant seems even more at home on Main Street today where increasingly diverse restaurants and shops have opened, including La Cocina del Puerco, Zizo's Greek and Mediterranean Market, Porcella Urban Market and Gilbert's Main Street Bagel and Deli.

Tested
Toy's Café Moo Shu Pork

1 pound pork, julienned
1 tablespoon minced garlic
1 tablespoon minced ginger
1 cup sliced shiitake mushrooms
2 cups shredded white cabbage
3/4 cup bamboo shoots, julienned (may use canned that have been rinsed well in cold water)
3/4 cup wood ear mushrooms, julienned (rehydrated)
1 cup hoisin-lime sauce
3 eggs, beaten lightly
1 bunch scallions, made into scallion brushes (to make brushes, hold scallion green and with a paring knife, make several vertical slices through white part. Immediately submerge in ice water and they will fan out, becoming "brushes")
4-6 chinese pancakes, steamed hot
Kosher salt and freshly cracked black pepper
Canola or grapeseed oil to cook

In a wok filled with 1 cup oil, bring to high temperature and add the pork. Using a strainer, quickly move around the pork and cook until medium rare, only 1 minute. Remove, strain pork and set aside.
Leave 2 tablespoons of oil in the wok and return to high heat. Add eggs to hot oil and scramble. Set them aside with cooked pork.
With remaining oil in wok, stir fry the garlic, ginger, and shiitake mushrooms until soft, about 2-3 minutes and season with kosher salt and freshly ground black pepper.
Add the cabbage, bamboo shoots, and wood ear mushrooms and continue stir frying 2-3 minutes.
Add half of the hoisin-lime and check for flavor.
Meanwhile, in a steamer, heat the pancakes until hot.
Lay individual pancakes on plates and paint on hoisin-lime sauce with the scallion brushes. Top with Moo-Shu, lay on 2 scallion brushes and roll up.
Yield: 4-6 pancakes

The Automobile Takes Bellevue on the Culinary Road
Car Culture and the Drive-In

In 1931, the community celebrated a new, paved highway connecting Bellevue to Renton and Seattle. Citizens rejoiced with a community picnic at Wildwood Park.[66] The highway development projects in the 1930's enabled Seattle residents to look to the Eastside for weekend or summertime outings. The allure of Bellevue's country environment and reasonably priced housing soon attracted many to move there permanently. Nevertheless, Seattle remained their workplace. Soon two bridges crossed Lake Washington to Bellevue. The Lacey V. Murrow Bridge opened in 1940, followed by the Albert D. Rossellini Bridge in 1963.[66]

Burgermaster, Kingen's, Dairy Queen, Dick's

The increasing fascination with the automobile created the new car culture. By the 1950's, everyone's activities involved their cars: teenagers cruised in them, families sat in them at the drive-in movie theatre, and "going out to eat" soon meant going to a drive-in restaurant. Fast food for those on a faster pace made sense. The Bellevue Burgermaster provides a nostalgic trip back to those early days. In 1967, the owners of the Seattle Burgermaster opened a Burgermaster in Bellevue near the Highway 520 and Bellevue Way intersection. Still operating today, the Drive-In continues to use carhops and the same menu featuring its time-honored hamburger with all the fixings and fries alongside a chocolate-flavored coke.[67]

Kingen's

In 1949, a new Bellevue high school opened south of Main Street. In 1955, Martha and Robert Kingen opened Kingen's, Bellevue's first Drive-In Restaurant at the corner of NE 8th and Bellevue Way. After school, teenagers loved to congregate at Kingen's for a coke and French fries. According to one Bellevue publication, at Kingen's you find "food and service fit for a King or Queen - and all the little Princes and Princesses."[68] The restaurant had a counter and a dining room, but customers also could stay in their cars and order from carhops. "We had a steady, returning clientele from the day we opened until the day we sold in 1960," said Martha Kingen in a 2006 interview. Before opening Kingen's, Robert Kingen served as a cook in the Navy. Following his service stint, he attended a cooking school on Broadway in Seattle.

The Kingen's son, Gerry, worked in his parents' restaurants, and in 1969 became the original owner of the first Red Robin located on the Montlake Cut in Seattle. The first burgers served there were his father's recipe for Kingen's famous King, Queen and Prince burgers. Robert Kingen also developed the seasoned salt used in Red Robin kitchens.[69]

Dairy Queen

The Bellevue Dairy Queen opened in 1961 at the corner of NE 8th and 112th Avenue NE. It remained there until April of 2006, when a developer bulldozed it for new construction, removing the familiar red-roofed hut from Bellevue's culinary landscape. Gene Morley, Bellevue franchise manager since 1981, remembers when the original Dairy Queen only sold the soft-frozen dessert, chocolate and vanilla with toppings; in the sixties the franchise introduced other food products, and the Bellevue store became known as the Dairy Queen/Brazier.

Dairy Queen came into being in 1939, created at "Sherb's", a small ice cream store in Kankakee, Illinois. The shops soon became the center of social life across small-town America. Today, the popular soft-frozen dairy product's official logo "DQ" shortens the original name.[70]

Dick's: Cold Ice Cream Mediates a Hot Topic

Dick Spady with two partners, H. Warren Ghormley and Dr. B.O.E. Thomas, founded Dick's Drive-In, their first restaurant, in 1954 in Wallingford, a Seattle district. The Bellevue Dick's opened in 1965, locating on the northeast corner of NE 10th and Bellevue Way; Coldwell Banker later built on the property. Moms with their kids came to the Bellevue Dick's, maybe in a Chevy II Nova station wagon, after swim lessons or before Scout and Campfire meetings. Teenagers arrived after school in noisy groups, a few fortunate enough to drive up in a sporty Ford Mustang. They came to Dick's for hamburgers, milk shakes and French fries. They wanted them quick, cheap and good. In 1965, a hamburger cost about 19 cents; a cheeseburger, 21cents; a coke, 10 cents; a milkshake, 21 cents; fries, 11 cents; a sundae, 24 cents and cones, 14 cents.[71]

Because the Bellevue location couldn't expand to accommodate parked cars, Dick's closed its Bellevue Drive-In restaurant after only a few years, but the chain still has restaurants in the Seattle area, making Dick's the longest operating locally owned fast food business in Washington.

While Dick's Drive-In still operated in Bellevue, it participated in an important community meeting held at the Bellevue Farrell's Ice Cream Parlour, on August 10, 1967, with representatives from the newly opened Eastside YMCA, the *Bellevue American* newspaper and 14 youths who also attended. The fourteen had been involved in disruptive incidents occurring at Dick's during the "long, hot summer." They all were eating ice cream sundaes, but the topic created a "heated" discussion. The YMCA agreed to organize a flag football league for the youths and the disruptiveness ended. Gathering around the table, eating ice cream, they found a positive solution for a community problem.[72]

Diversifying Food Traditions 1970 to 1990

Bellevue's Changing Culinary Tradition

Following the middle years of the twentieth century, the soft edges of Bellevue's gracious suburban lifestyle faded. The process accelerated after August 28, 1963, when Washington's Governor, Albert Rosellini, cut the ribbon inaugurating the completion of the second floating bridge across Lake Washington, a link between Seattle's Montlake District and the Evergreen Point in Medina.[1]

A significant culinary influence occurred in the 1960's when Julia Child published *Mastering the Art of French Cooking*, a book that revolutionized the way Americans thought about food. Child inaugurated her nationwide television program, "The French Chef," in 1963. Americans became enthusiastic about learning new ways of cooking and about food and wine.[2]

During this era, Bellevue's culinary traditions were modified with some interesting additions. The Washington wine industry established itself, as did Bellevue's first cooking school, kitchen and wine shops. Families celebrated birthdays, but often they preferred to go out to Farrell's, a "pseudo-vintage" ice cream parlor. Specialty groceries and shops opened alongside the national fast food franchises proliferating in small community shopping areas and in downtown Bellevue. The annual Arts and Crafts fairs continued to thrive, and, in 1975, the community proudly opened the Bellevue Art Museum in the former Green's Chapel of Flowers on Bellevue Way. As health and fitness became a concern, the Bellevue Club, built in 1979, provided a new venue for community club breakfasts and business lunches. Community events and celebrations took the form of receptions, rather than picnics and banquets.

By the 1980's, people came from all over the world to work in the tech industry located on the Eastside. In 1983, Microsoft began operations close to Northup Way and held so many lunch and dinner meetings at nearby Bravo Pagliaccio that the restaurant became known as the "Microsoft cafeteria." Many settled east of the Bellevue's downtown core, and, in response to the increasingly diverse surrounding community, Crossroads Shopping Center developed a "market" concept with ethnic restaurants and live music entertainment. A more complex and vibrant way of life overtook Bellevue, the result of accelerating growth and development. It eventually gained economic and political independence and the status of an "Edge City."[3]

Julia Child's Food Revolution

In the 1950's and 1960's, Bellevue children, as children elsewhere in the United States, grew up eating many of the same recipes: tuna casserole with canned mushroom soup, chicken with canned peas, macaroni with Wisconsin cheddar cheese, frozen TV dinners, Jello, glazed ham for holiday dinners, hamburgers and hotdogs. If their parents chose to drink alcoholic beverages, they drank cocktails.[4]

Julia Child 1971 Frederick & Nelson Demonstration

Julia Child came to the Northwest, already well known for her nationally syndicated column that appeared in the *Seattle Post-Intelligencer*. Time magazine had featured her on its November 25, 1966, cover.[5] In 1971, Child came to the Seattle Frederick & Nelson to autograph copies of her *Mastering the Art of French Cooking Volume II* and to give a demonstration. Child encouraged both the craft of cooking and a respect for good food, informing the public with her books and her public and television appearances. She inspired American entrepreneurs like Chuck Williams, who opened a chain of kitchen shops, and Nancy Lazara, who opened Bellevue's first cooking school.

The New Tools for Cooking

Only a few kitchen stores existed in the United States before Chuck Williams opened Williams-Sonoma in 1956. Williams made French copper and cooking utensils available in his West Coast stores and, beginning in 1971, nationwide through his catalogues. Before the specialized kitchen shop, many towns across America relied on hardware and other general stores for kitchen and housewares. In the 1950's, these stores primarily stocked aluminum pie plates and cooking pans and cast iron skillets.[6] To expand and improve their culinary skills, America's aspiring cooks and chefs needed better tools and cooking classes to make the transition Julia Child had envisioned for them.

Chez Nancy Cooking Classes

By the age of 15, Nancy Lazara already knew she wanted to make cooking her profession. She read a magazine article, "Mastering the Art of Choosing a Cooking School" written by Julia Child, who recommended the London Cordon Bleu School "if what you want to do is learn to cook." Nancy followed her advice and in 1971 enrolled in the London school for a year, receiving her Cordon Bleu diploma. Nancy credits Julia Child for generating interest in cooking and food in America. "There was always a frenzy to get her cookbooks when she published one."[7] Julia Child's 1974 benefit appearance at Seattle's Saint Mark's Cathedral helped focus interest on Pacific Northwest cuisine as did her interest in Northwest food and wine. Child took note of Bellevue vintner Paul Thomas' wines: "We have enjoyed all of your wines, but I think I like the Crimson Rhubarb particularly."[8]

The Yankee Kitchen

After Julia Child's Saint Mark Cathedral's benefit, Nancy Lazara established her own cooking school, Chez Nancy, on 102nd Avenue NE in downtown Bellevue in 1975.

It was the first private cooking school in Bellevue and became such a success that her mother, Carol Lazara, decided to buy the Yankee Kitchen on Main Street. From 1977 to 1985, Nancy and her mother ran the Yankee Kitchen shop and offered cooking classes, eventually expanding to accommodate a staff of eight teachers.

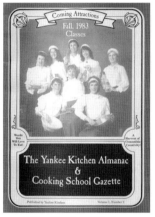

The most popular classes were "Cooking Seafood," the "Basics of Cooking," and "Easy Entertaining." Celebrity chefs, among them, Madeleine Kamman, well known for her Massachusetts cooking school cookbooks, appeared at the Bellevue store. The Yankee Kitchen cooking school influenced what went on the table in Bellevue's homes, both because so many local homemakers trained in them, and because they became a magnet for visiting celebrity chefs and area teachers.

According to Nancy Lazara, "Bellevue's berries, natural ingredients and informal style of entertaining, informal fun on a boat or at home, epitomized the Northwest and its culinary traditions." After selling the Yankee Kitchen, Nancy Lazara became director of food services for Larry's Markets stores. She currently uses her culinary skills in the product development field for Starbucks and comments, "Today's cooks are looking more for short cuts and new products make that possible; you even can buy a demi-glace sauce in a can today."[9]

Jeanette Sullivan, Seattle caterer and restaurateur, taught cooking classes at the Yankee Kitchen. In an interview in 2005 she recalled, "People were so eager to learn. Most students wanted to learn for personal not professional reasons." She credits Julia Child with coming "along at the right time when Americans were ready to be interested in food." Sullivan adds, "However, I learned more from Nancy Lazara than anyone. She was so natural in front of the public and on the TV morning talk shows."[10]

"The Yankee Kitchen Almanac and Cooking School Gazette" Fall, 1983

New kitchen tools and products influenced cooking class curriculum. "When Starbucks opened it was a major event to buy a coffee grinder and the coffee beans. If a specialty store like DeLaurenti's started selling yogurt and other previously unavailable items, classes evolved with these new products."[11]

Nancy Lazara recommends this recipe, one that she taught in her cooking school, because it looks pretty and fresh. It can be made up to three days ahead of time and is easy to assemble. "You just pour the cake ingredients on the counter and mash them together."[9]

French Style - Danish Strawberry Cake
Nancy Lazara, Food Specialist, Teacher, and Consultant

2 cups plus 2 tablespoons flour
6 ounces butter (3/4 cup)
2/3 cup of confectioner's sugar
2 egg yolks
few drops vanilla
strawberries
strawberry jelly
whipped cream

Preheat oven to 375 degrees F.
Sift flour onto a pastry board or marble slab. Make a large well in the center. Pour in sugar, butter, egg yolks and vanilla. Work the ingredients in the well into a smooth paste with the fingers. Gradually draw in the flour and knead gently until smooth.

Wrap the dough in cheese cloth or waxed paper and chill at least 1 hour.
Put on a baking sheet and pat out into a round shape, 1/2 -inch thick, taking care to leave room on the sheet around the edges for the dough to expand. Prick the cake all over and flute the edges.

Bake for 20 - 25 minutes, until barely golden brown. Cool on a rack.
Cover with whole strawberries. Brush the berries with boiling hot strawberry jelly.
Chill. Just before serving, decorate with rosettes of whipped cream.
Yield: Serves 4 to 6. Can be doubled or tripled.

Mr. J's Culinary Essentials

In 1977, Larry Jaffe opened a kitchen shop next to Swensen's Ice Cream Factory on NE 8th. In 1984, he moved the shop to its present QFC Bellevue Village location. Looking at the history of Mr. J's provides a window on the changing tastes and culinary needs of Bellevue homemakers and amateur chefs.

In the early years, Mr. J's was known for its selections of silverware and dinnerware; Fitz & Floyd, Dansk, and Arabia were especially popular brands. Larry Jaffe, good at recognizing trends, realized that Bellevue customers were shifting to less formal entertaining and more diverse cuisines, so he began phasing out the dinnerware. After Jaffe died in the year 2000, his wife, Debbie, revamped the store, bringing in Vietri, a Tuscan line of table and cooking ware. She stocks the store with

Mr. J's Culinary Essentials Kitchen Shop

hard-to-find culinary items. Debbie Jaffe says that TV's cooking channel generates a renewed interest in kitchens, even inspiring men who come to the shop to buy a special utensil because they want to cook a television recipe. Jaffe, a supporter of the Bellevue Farmers Market, believes in the benefits of home cooking because it is ". . . fresh and healthy and a way to encourage families to gather around the table."[12]

Pacific Northwest Cuisine and Cookbooks: Sharon Kramis

Sharon Kramis has fond memories of Bellevue's Overlake Blueberry Farm and Gilham's Garden south of Lake Hills, annual childhood summer destinations. Her love for Northwest foods grew into a culinary career that includes authoring regional cookbooks, giving food demonstrations, and being a restaurant consultant for Anthony's restaurants over the past twenty-five years. Kramis appeared at sold-out demonstrations at the Bellevue Club, sharing recipes for Northwest cranberry sauce with Grand Marnier and hazelnut or pistachio biscotti.

In the 1970's, Kramis honed her cooking skills in James Beard's classes. She and her family took their summer vacations in Seaside, Oregon, for her to attend Beard's annual classes there. She says, "Beard was a huge influence. His love of straightforward food, seasonal and regional; this was the beginning by definition of Northwest cuisine." Northwest cooks learned from him that applying good culinary practices can only succeed with "extraordinary," preferably local, ingredients.[13]

In 1988, Kramis coauthored a cookbook with Schuyler Ingle entitled *Northwest Bounty: The Extraordinary Foods and Wonderful Cooking of the Pacific Northwest*. The cookbook includes chapters entitled Seafood, Shellfish, Berries, Tree Fruit and The Wines and Spirits of the Northwest. Extensive descriptions of ingredients and their sources appear along with helpful suggestions that whet the appetite both for eating and cooking: "Cherries: Bing: Crisp, wine-red or black. Great for eating fresh. When dried, these work well in sauces. Rainier: Yellow-red in color. Sweet, apple-crisp. For cooking and canning as well as eating fresh."[14] See Kramis' cookbook, *Berries: A Country Garden Cookbook*, for Willy's Blackberry Crisp, a very delicious fruit crisp recipe.

Junior League Cookbooks Benefit Bellevue

The Junior League of Seattle provides volunteer docents, and proceeds from Junior League of Seattle Cookbooks give financial support for children's programs sponsored by the Bellevue Arts Museum. Starting in 1985, Culture Cube exposed Eastside children to art with a hands-on approach, introducing them to Northwest Art such as contemporary weavings and Native American pieces. Other beneficiaries of Junior League funds and volunteer time include Youth Eastside Services, the Eastside Domestic Violence Program and Eastside Community Mental Health Center.

While JLS cookbooks rejoice in food, League members have always proven sensitive and responsive to community needs such as hunger and preventable childhood diseases. Starting in 1994, League volunteers held Baby Boost Information Fairs in Bellevue and other Eastside cities. Infant formula, baby food, critical items like diapers, blankets, toothbrushes as well as health information were provided free for client families of the Eastside Multiservice Centers. To maximize impact of the Baby Boost fairs, the Junior League also provided translation services, as many families did not speak English. With their cookbook endeavors, JLS now sponsors healthy eating among children.

The JLS Mission Statement reads: The Junior League of Seattle is an organization of women committed to promoting voluntarism, developing the potential of women and improving the community through the effective action and leadership of trained volunteers. Its purpose is exclusively educational and charitable.[15] (Reprinted with the permission of the Junior League of Seattle.)

Celebrating Ice Cream and Cake

We can thank the colonists for bringing along their ice cream recipes when they

crossed the seas to America. References to ice cream occur throughout American culinary history. Ice cream appeared in advertisements in *The Lake Washington Reflector* in the first part of the twentieth century. During those years, Bellevue citizens churned their own ice cream in the summer and bought cones in grocery stores or at Meta Burrows' soda fountain on Main Street.[16]

After World War II, Dairy Queen and other soft frozen dessert products eclipsed the popularity of premium ice cream. Ice cream parlors and soda fountains virtu-

Frederick & Nelson Sundae

ally disappeared, and premium ice creams did not regain popularity until the 1970's.[17] In Bellevue, ice cream desserts began to revive with Farrell's and other specialty ice cream chains.

Farrell's Ice Cream Parlor

Farrell's brought back the old-time ice cream parlor just when families, less inclined to bake a cake and serve it with ice cream at home, were ready to go out to celebrate birthdays. At the Bellevue Village Farrell's, the whole wait staff entertained, along with other customers. The staff blew a horn, marched out and created a fanfare singing "Happy Birthday" at the same time presenting a fantastic dessert to the birthday child, or adult. In 1963 Bob Farrell opened the first Farrell's Ice Cream Parlour in Portland, Oregon. His tagline was "Farrell's Features Fabulous Food and Fantastic Fountain Fantasies for Frolicking Fun-Filled Festive Families." Farrell's eventually opened 130 parlors throughout the United States.[18]

Swensen's Ice Cream Factory

In 1977, Paul Jaffe opened a Swensen's Old Fashioned Ice Cream Factory franchise in downtown Bellevue. When the shop first opened, a single scoop cost 35 cents, later 50 cents. When they raised it to 75 cents, Jaffe thought, "No one will buy one scoop for 75 cents!" Customers especially enjoyed looking into an adjoining room through a viewing window to watch the process of making the ice cream. Jaffe only sold the recipes Swensen's developed, but had fun experimenting a little with his own flavors. As for the ice cream business? "It was a lot of fun while it lasted!" Jaffe sold the franchise in 1981.[19]

Remembrances: Growing Up In Bellevue

Marvel Morgan circa 1969

Kyle D. Fulwiler: "There was Farrell's that we went to where the [Bellevue Village] QFC now exists." We used to get giant sundaes and banana splits. I think they had the special for a whole group that was a giant bowl of ice cream carried in by two people on shoulder racks. [Editor's note: Farrell's specialty, known as the "Zoo Sundae" cost $8.95 in 1971.] The big sundae was called the "Mount Rainier." It fed around ten people, and if you ordered it and ate it by yourself, you got it free. A friend of ours did this. When I was a teenager, it was the "in" ice cream place."

Gail Round: "Marvel Morgan's had an ice cream parlor inside the store, and they had these ice cream cones that held three scoops parallel to each other. There was another ice cream parlor called Swensen's. You would go in and order your ice cream; it was placed in a paper cone in a stainless steel holder. There also was the soda fountain at Newberry's in Bellevue Square, and you could buy a five-cent ice cream cone at Albertsons."[20]

Kyle D. Fulwiler, a "daughter" of Bellevue, went on to become chef at the Governor's Mansion in Olympia and offers this recipe.

Tested
Apple Dumplings

Better than apple pie! The rich, lovely apple taste is worth the preparation time. Note: Using a whole apple sliced part way holds the shape of the dumpling.

Crust
1 3/4 cup unbleached white flour
1 pinch salt
6 ounces butter cut into 1/2 -inch pieces

1/4 cup cold water
Filling
4 apples (3 cups of Gravenstein or Granny Smith)
3 cups water
1/2 cup sugar
2 teaspoons cinnamon
1/2 cup sugar

Preheat oven 425 degrees F.

Place the flour and salt in the bowl of a food processor and add the butter. Process this mixture until it is very fine, a little coarser than cornmeal. Add the water and process until a ball of dough is just beginning to form. Turn food processor bowl upside down onto a flour-covered surface and remove the dough. Gently knead a couple of times to form the ball. Wrap in plastic wrap and chill for 30 minutes.

Peel and core apples, reserving peels. Thinly slice apples and set aside. Place peels in a saucepan with water and 1/2 cup sugar; bring to a boil, then simmer 20 minutes and strain. Meanwhile, roll out dough into a rectangle and cut it into six 5-inch squares. Divide slices (or whole apples) evenly and arrange on each square. Sprinkle squares with cinnamon and remaining 1/2 cup sugar. Seal each square around apples by pinching pastry together. Place dumplings in a deep buttered baking dish. Pour enough apple peel liquid into dish to cover dumplings halfway. Bake for 40 minutes, basting once.
Yield: 6-8 dumplings.

From Birthday Cakes to Catering to the Multitudes

It started with cakes. Jean McClure, capable entrepreneur, exemplifies many women of her era who used their skills to serve Bellevue and build the community, going beyond traditional roles. McClure, a mother of three daughters and a substitute teacher, founded Kakes and Kookies for Kollege Kids after reading about the idea in a popular magazine. For a year, she baked birthday cakes and cookies and delivered them to out-of-state students attending the University of Washington. Families and friends, who lived too far to help their student celebrate, paid Jean $3.50 for a cake. She barely broke even after driving across the Evergreen Point Bridge to deliver the cake, paying the 35-cent toll and with the cost of ingredients and gas. Nevertheless, in her words, she "had fun," and her endeavor led her to learn cake decorating and the art of food presentation.

She then became a founder of the 4-M's Catering with three other Bellevue cooks whose names began with the letter M: McDonald, Meyer and Magnuson. From 1969 to 1974, Jean McClure organized the weekly dinner for the Bellevue First Presbyterian Youth Group. "You have to know the price of things to be successful," she says. When her budget permitted it, she ordered hamburgers from the Bellevue Dick's Drive-In. McClure wrote *You Can Feed the Multitudes, Too*, a cookbook with recipes and meal ideas for large groups. McClure eventually gave up the Youth Group but continued the catering services until 2005.[21]

With three daughters who were members of Camp Fire Girls, Jean McClure discovered ways to use the Camp Fire mints they sold annually and accumulated in her freezer. Sometimes she used them as a frosting on top of Brownies, or she used the mints to make what she called "Winter Style S'Mores." In the 1920's, the Girl Scouts described in their camping handbook the recipe for S'Mores, so-named because it's difficult not to ask for "some more" of this gooey campfire desert, especially when seated around the campfire.[22]

Heritage Recipe
Camp Fire Mint S'Mores "Winter Style"
Jean McClure

One graham cracker per person
Top graham cracker with a dollar-size Camp Fire mint
Top mint with a marshmallow

For a traditional S'More, toast a marshmallow over a campfire, place the hot, melting marshmallow on a piece of chocolate that tops a graham cracker so the chocolate melts onto the cookie base. In the wintertime, place the assembled S'Mores on a cookie sheet under the oven broiler. Watch them carefully, and when the marshmallow begins to brown remove from the oven and serve, open-faced or as a "sandwich," putting a second graham cracker on the top, pressing together the melted chocolate and marshmallow.

Bellevue's Grape Story

Currant Wine

The Northwest has a long tradition of wine making. Jacqueline Williams, Northwest culinary historian, reports that pioneers made wine from currants. She provides this 1871 recipe: The winemaker combines 3 quarts currants with 3 pounds sugar and 3 quarts "soft" water. After allowing fermentation, "Close it up, if in a keg, if in a jar, bottle it."[23]

The Summit Winery

The moderate northwest climate conducive to growing tree fruits and berries naturally led to the cultivation of grapes in Bellevue. Robert and Mary Borg purchased a 10-acre tract of land on the top of Clyde Hill in 1923.

Hennig's Grapes

They cultivated Island Belle grapes and made wine by aging the juice in five-gallon barrels. The Borgs maintained their vineyard until 1943.[24]

Hennig Grapes

In 1920, John Clarke began growing acres of grapes off 100th Avenue NE, not

far from the Borg property. From Clarke, Adolph Hennig purchased a five-acre tract with a three-acre vineyard and later expanded it to eight acres.[25] By 1924, Hennig developed equipment to make grape juice for sale, annually selling about 12,000 gallons to grocery stores from Bellingham to Olympia under the labels: Hennig's Grape Juice, Red and White brand and Old Homestead brand. Adolph's son,

Hennig's Grape Juice Label circa 1920

Robert, remembers that during the Depression years they sold it on consignment.[26]

Hennig recalls that during Prohibition in the 1920's, home winemakers came to Hennig's family grape vineyard to buy grapes to make wine. When World War II created a labor shortage and the Hennigs needed help harvesting their grapes, a Seattle winemaker and his extended Italian family came to pick the Hennig's grapes for wine. The family sold the vineyard in 1951; a few grape vines continue to grow on the west side of the property.[27]

Heritage Recipe
Grape Juice Dessert
Robert Hennig

Heat grape juice and thicken it with tapioca.
Serve with "real" whipped cream.

"Thank goodness the spray canned whipped cream had not been invented yet!" Robert Hennig exclaimed.

Prohibition

Prohibition created dry years between 1919 and 1933, banning the manufacture, sale, and transport of alcoholic beverages. Vintners turned to making grape juice or converted their fields to the production of raisins. An early attempt to arouse the dormant wine industry occurred when Secretary of State William J. Crockett, a member of President Lyndon Johnson's administration, 1963 to 1969, ordered domestic wines to be served at official U.S. functions.[28]

Food and Wine at Pete's

Because of Washington State law, for many years merchants could sell wine only as an adjunct to food in grocery stores. In addition, taxes on wines produced outside the state discouraged importation of European or California wines. In the 1960's, only a dozen wineries operated in the state, and people did not know much about wine, choosing to drink beer or mixed drinks.[29]

In 1969, George Kingen operated the Lakeshore Mini-Mart in Seattle's Madison Park district. He sold both wine and food, and customers ordered wines from him that he purchased at the State liquor store. At the same time he picked up specialty wines to sell, buying at retail prices until 1969 when laws changed, and distributors began selling wines. The elimination of restrictions on selling wines, increased education about food and wines, and increasing international travel helped to open the Washington wine barrel spigot that has been flowing ever since.

In 1991, Kingen and his wife, Sue, opened Pete's Wines in Bellevue. Wine preferences differ store to store. The Bellevue Pete's sells 130 different champagne labels and stocks more Chardonnay than the Lake Union Pete's. The Bellevue Pete's contributes to local charities, most recently to the Forgotten Children's Fund and the Boys and Girls Club.[30]

La Cantina: Wines for Bellevue's Celebrations

La Cantina began as a one-store family wine shop in Seattle, one of the first to open following the repeal of protectionist wine laws. Larry Alhadeff bought it and created a small local chain of wine shops including, in 1974, one in Bellevue on NE 8th near 102nd Avenue NE. La Cantina was Bellevue's first wine shop.

In 1975, Tom Cottrell became its manager and, ten years later, its owner. Long fascinated by the history of the wine countries and intrigued by the lifestyle connected with wine and food, Cottrell loves and knows wine. Cottrell began selling California wines when the exchange rates no longer favored French wines. Washington soon had its own wineries. In the 1980's, 80 Washington State wineries operated; by 2006, close to 500. Unlike wineries, wine shops cannot legally donate wine for public benefits and events. Nonetheless, La Cantina has contributed much to community celebrations with in-kind advice and guidance for planning weddings, anniversaries, parties and civic events.[31]

Paul Thomas Winery

It seems fitting that internationally acclaimed winemaker Paul Thomas established his winery in Bellevue, a town whose first identity came from the cultivation of strawberries. Thomas made his reputation from fruit wines, prizewinning fruit wines, that, in the words of noted wine authority Anthony Dias Blue, created a new world category of wines. Thomas created upscale fruit wines that could be served on

the finest tables with the highest quality foods.

At the peak of production, Thomas produced 25,000 cases of wine in his Bellevue winery located at 1717 136th Place NE. The Bellevue winery with its well-appointed wood-paneled tasting room became the site of many events, including benefit dinners for the Fred Hutchinson Hospital. Dinners with wine proved to be popular auction items for good causes; people who attended began to appreciate wine before it gained economic importance in the Northwest. Thomas showed them how wine as an extension of the food experience can add to the dining experience.

Paul Thomas' talents partly can be traced to his family's more than 100 years of Northwest agricultural history. His grandfather planted orchards in 1905, and in 1933, his father began exporting apples overseas. Thomas says, "My mother is the real farmer. She could pick out a good watermelon just from its smell." Paul Thomas inherited his mother's sensitivities and applied them to winemaking.

Thomas also credits a trip to France in 1960 and says he "never got over it." He lived in Spain for a while, and because of similar climate and growing conditions, he believed that Washington State would become a major center for viniculture. For about ten years, while he taught school, he made his own fruit wines. He wanted to do something different with wines. Before Thomas, fruit wines had the reputation for being too sweet, but his were different, and wine connoisseurs around the world began to take notice. He produced wines made from crimson rhubarb, Bing cherries and Bartlett pears, and he discovered how well they complimented certain foods. The Bartlett pear wines paired nicely with Asian cuisines and the rhubarb wine went well with broiled salmon. Every year, *The Seattle Times* wine columnist, Tom Stockley, promoted the Paul Thomas Bing cherry wine as the perfect wine to serve with Thanksgiving turkey.

In 1990, Thomas sold his winery, and the Bellevue winery and tasting room moved to Sunnyside, Washington. Thomas has no regrets. He and his wife Judy spend happy hours tending their beautiful gardens, and, presumably, enjoying a glass of Paul Thomas fruit wine from time to time.[32]

The "Italian Wave"

Bravo Pagliaccio

Dorene Centioli McTigue has been associated with Italian cuisine all of her life.

Her grandparents emigrated from Italy to Seattle, bringing with them their love of Italian food. For many years, her Grandmother DeCaro operated a grocery store in Seattle. McTigue's father, Gil Centioli, opened Gil's Drive-In in Bellevue in 1960, and he eventually owned thirty Kentucky Fried Chicken franchises in Washington State. After receiving a journalism degree from Seattle

University, McTigue worked in her father's office.

She always wanted to have her own restaurant, and in 1979, she opened a take-out Pagliacci Pizza by the Slice in the University District. In 1981, she opened a second one on Broadway, expanding it with a trattoria menu and table service. McTigue took cooking classes in New York and Venice, Italy. In 1982 and 1983, she attended classes from Marcella Hazan, who taught master classes on Italian cuisine and wrote cookbooks.

In 1984, she opened Bravo Pagliaccio near Highway 520 and Bellevue Way. According to McTigue, Bravo had the first wood-burning pizza oven in the Northwest constructed according to specifications of the oven builder for Chez Panisse, Alice Waters' innovative Berkeley restaurant. Although some restaurants already used fresh string pasta, McTigue was the first to make ravioli and tortellini on-site. She brought in new products like Taleggio cheese that she sliced, bundled in grape leaves and tied with scallions and baked in the wood-fired oven.

"At Bravo we offered a sophisticated menu. We could seat 240 with our two banquet rooms. Microsoft had offices across the street. Bill Gates came in with bankers and made a lot of

Bravo Paggliaccio Pizza Chef circa 1980

deals in our banquet rooms. They called us "Microsoft's Cafeteria".

McTigue closed Bravo in 1993. Delivery pizza was a big thing then, so she opened fifteen Pagliacci Pizza Kitchens, three on the Eastside, including Bridal Trails and Crossroads. In 2001, she sold Pagliacci, but retains ownership of the property where she operated Bravo Pagliaccio. She loved being in the restaurant business, because she loved the people, the people she worked with and the people she served. She calls it a "people business, not a food business." As for the future culinary world, she predicts that the "Star" chef will come to an end as chefs become more involved in food production. Bellevue can claim Dorene Centioli McTigue as a "star" of its own culinary history. Bravo![33]

Café Juanita and Cavatappi Wine

In 1977, Peter Dow opened Café Juanita in Kirkland. He had worked in several restaurants and always liked food and cooking. "It gave me both a job and something to eat," he says. For residents in Bellevue and Seattle, Dow's restaurant became a destination where they celebrated special occasions. Dow's restaurant also helped further define, with Italian influences, Northwest cuisine.

The "Italian wave" had begun its influence on American cuisine, and he became curious about Italian food. He made fresh pasta, a new idea to entice Northwest diners. That and other recipes featuring Northwest ingredients with Italian influences attracted newspaper reviews. The restaurant soon became "crazy" famous, to use Dow's words.

They used a blackboard menu so they could be more flexible when prices changed.

Dow remembers that when they first opened, Pollo ai Pistacchio was listed at $4.75 and 25 years later was selling for $14.00. He learned that with wine, people don't always choose the cheapest on the list. He offered a Casarsa wine for $4.00, but no one chose it. He raised the price to $6.00, and, finally, after he charged $9.00, it became so popular that he could sell a case a week.

While traveling in Italy, he discovered that many restaurants had their own wineries. He started making wine, and in 1985 officially bonded his own winery, naming it Cavatappi Italian for corkscrew. He sold Café Juanita to Holly Smith in April of 2000. He thinks she has taken the restaurant to a much higher level than he was able to and is pleased she is doing such a great job with it. As for current and future culinary trends, he notes the interest in healthier foods and Pacific Rim cuisines. He also believes we have to face new challenges to feed the world's growing population.[34]

Cooking Imports Special Events and Moments

DeLaurenti's: The Specialty Grocer

Cheeses: fontina and parmesan for pasta; feta and goat for salads; or brie and camembert, just for eating with fruit; everyone who shopped at DeLaurenti's came because no one else sold such a variety of fresh cheeses and specialty items. They came to DeLaurenti's for pastas, beans, spices and wines, too, but almost always for the cheeses.

In 1946, Pete and Mamie DeLaurenti opened Pete's Specialty Foods in Seattle's Pike Street Market. One son, Lewis, known to everyone as Louie, eventually became owner of DeLaurenti's Specialty Foods.

Bellevue DeLaurenti Store   Between 1945 and 1975, "Greek and Italian patrons often came in with spouses recently arrived from Europe, and they searched for foods from their homelands," the DeLaurentis recalled. In 1976, he opened a second store in Bellevue on Bellevue Way next to Downtown Park. A family enterprise, Louie's wife, Pat, became store manager, and daughters, Vicki and Kandi, often helped behind the counter.

In the early years, they traveled to food shows in Europe to find the products they wanted to sell, olive oil and balsamic vinegar, a wide selection of spices, French and Greek cheeses, wines and deli meats. At the Bellevue store, they frequently served clients who had moved from the East Coast and were accustomed to specialty and ethnic food stores. Some came to the store weekly to buy the cheeses *DeLaurenti Advertisement* and condiments they needed. Air freight made imported foods more available and affordable, and meant the DeLaurentis could supply their stores more easily.

In Bellevue in the mid-1980's, Bellevue Square's reconstruction as an enclosed mall changed shopping habits, discouraging shoppers from "moving around town to shop," according to DeLaurenti. However, by the 1990's, customers, motivated by cooking shows, food magazines and diversely ethnic and upscale restaurants, frequented specialty stores like DeLaurenti's.[35]

Heritage Recipe
Panna Cotta

Louie DeLaurenti calls this his favorite dessert. The recipe produces a traditional panna cotta dessert. Enjoy with fresh fruit on the side.
1 cup whole milk
1 cup heavy cream (whipping cream)
1/4 cup sugar
2 sheets gelatin or 1 1/2 teaspoons gelatin (1/2 packet)

Heat milk, heavy cream and sugar and simmer for 15 minutes. Place gelatin sheets in shallow bowl and cover with warm water, or if using gelatin powder, sprinkle over 2 tablespoons of the cream. Remove simmered milk and cream from heat and add gelatin. For the gelatin sheets, squeeze and add to cream mixture. If you use powdered gelatin, add to mixture. Stir to dissolve thoroughly.

Strain 1/2 cup of each of the next mixture into four lightly buttered molds and refrigerate for 4 to 6 hours. To serve, run a knife around edge and unmold panna cotta onto individual serving plates. Fresh or frozen fruits and a dollop of whipped cream may be added for your presentation. Panna Cotta may also be served in individual ramekins or goblets (do not butter molds).

For the company's 100th anniversary in 2003 the Magnano family changed the Napoleon label, replacing the original imperial portrait of Napoleon Bonaparte with a younger Napoleon and the words "1903 Classic Taste 2003" - "Family owned in the Northwest."

The Napoleon Co. 1912-1913
A. Magnano Importer of Fancy Groceries
Grocery Price List
Seattle WA Vancouver BC

Reggiano or Parmesan, 4 cheese in a tub, about 200 lb. 36¢ per lb.
Eels - smoked - per dozen $3.50
Napoleon Brand Olive Oil Extra Virgin per gallon $2.75
Italian Cigars - Napolitani and Toscani shapes
in boxes of 100 cigars per 1,000 $13

Bellevue Importing Firm

Antonio Magnano founded an importing company, The Napoleon Co., in 1903, conducting business in a building on Fourth Avenue South and Atlantic Street in Seattle. In 1988, the Napoleon Co. moved to Bellevue where it remains a family owned, locally operated company. Magnano started his business when immigrants to Seattle were primarily from Europe and demanded European products. More than one hundred years later, residents of Bellevue and Seattle increasingly come from all over the world and demand a wider variety of imported foods; they also prefer natural and organic foods.

Antonio's grandson and company president Joe Magnano travels all over the world seeking the best products to import: paprika from Hungary, olive oils from Italy and Spain and other specialty items. Magnano has to adapt the business to regional tastes, noting that his West Coast customers prefer artichokes canned in oil like canola. He also has to consider world currencies and free trade policy challenges. Food imports create connections for Bellevue home cooks and restaurateurs wishing to express their culinary artistry. The Napoleon Co. imported products array Bellevue's supermarket and specialty food store shelves, offering new ways to interpret the local culinary story.[36]

Friends Meet at the Lake Hills' Liebchen Delicatessen

Lake Hills, a small community shopping center east of Downtown Bellevue, can claim a bit of culinary fame as the site of the first QFC, opened in 1956. In addition, the Liebchen Delicatessan has operated there since 1971, a German-style delicatessen that would be typical in Europe but provides unique meats, salads and imported goods not usually available in Bellevue.

A steady stream of customers arrives at the Lake Hills Liebchen Delicatessen throughout the day to purchase bratwurst and cervelets, hot German mustard and sauerkraut. At the holidays, the come to choose a Christmas stollen. Friends meet at the Liebchen; after all, "liebchen" is German for "sweetheart" or "darling." Sometimes they order a sandwich and coffee with homemade potato salad to eat at one of two little tables.

Lynne Rosenthal, owner since it opened in 1971, knows many of her customers by name and what they have on their shopping list. "Two-thirds of our customers are western Europeans and most live in Lake Hills and the Crossroads area of Bellevue. The Bavarian

Liebchen Delicatessan

Delicatessen at the Pike Street Market prepares some of my meats, others I order from New York, and my order hasn't changed much since the 1970's. I have just enhanced the quantities."

The Liebchen Delicatessen celebrated its 35th anniversary at Octoberfest in 2006 with live music and food. Tucked away in a little corner of Bellevue, the German delicatessen serves a tasty bite of Europe with the loving care of its dedicated proprietor. Lynne Rosenthal adds proudly, "We aren't unique. We're typical for a German delicatessen."[37]

Brenner Brothers Bakery: Bakery-Deli Pioneer

When Brenner Brothers Bakery closed in 1996, for Bellevue it meant the loss of fresh-baked braided challah breads, blintzes, and bagels with lox. The bakery-deli combination, unusual when the Bellevue store opened in 1969, became a popular gathering place for Jewish families and other customers who came for a lunch of matzo ball soup or Brenner's prize-winning pastrami sandwich and a piece of chocolate cream pie, all for a good price.

When Alan Brenner closed the Bellevue Brenner Brothers, for the Seattle area it meant the end of the ninety-year history for the family owned bakery enterprise. Alan Brenner's grandfather came to Seattle by train in 1901 and walked up Yesler until he found a boarding house. He eventually married the daughter of the woman who ran the boarding house. He opened a bakery, first at 18th and Yesler, and then one on Cherry Street. All the children worked in the bakery. Alan's father, Charles, born in 1919, remembers sweeping the floors and collecting wood for the wood stove to boil water in the bagel pot.

In 1969, when their father died, and there was increasing unrest in the Central District, the Brenner family, including Joe, Charley and Itsey Brenner, and their sister Jetta, opened Brenner Brothers Bakery on 120th Avenue NE in Bellevue. Although the bakery closed in 1996, Brenner Brothers breads remain on many grocery shelves, baked at a Federal Way location.[38]

Specialty Supermarket: The Bellevue Uwajimaya

UWAJIMAYA *Since 1928* ✿   Fujimatsu Moriguchi went into business in 1928 selling Japanese fish cakes in Tacoma, Washington. He named his first store after Uwajima, Japan, calling it Uwajimaya; "ya" means store. After World War II he opened a retail store in Seattle.

In the 1970's, Japanese families coming to the Seattle area to work for Japanese multinational companies often settled in Bellevue where they joined a long-established Japanese population. Recognizing the business opportunity in Bellevue, in 1978, the company opened the Uwajimaya store on NE 24th Street between Bellevue-Redmond Road and 156th Avenue NE. In the early years they offered primarily Japanese retail and food items, but later began to include products for customers wanting ingredients from other Asian cuisines. The Uwajimaya Asian food court provides a place to meet and to eat hot and cold prepared Asian foods, to purchase food to take home and to learn about Asian tradition, products and wares.

Alan Kurimura, Company Representative, states, "We are on the Eastside to stay and are very appreciative of the loyalty of our customers. We focus on high quality and a variety of seafood and Asian produce." The Japanese community has been an important part of the culinary heritage of Bellevue since the early 1900's, when Japanese farmers planted its famous strawberry fields. Uwajimaya continues the historical timeline, enriching the palate and cuisine of the Eastside as well as its community life of shared traditions.[39]

Catering to Health

As Americans began to appreciate food in general and regional cuisines in particular, they also became aware of the connection between food and health. Health clubs opened, and menus offered more healthy options. Asian cuisines appealed to the health conscious because of the emphasis on vegetables and fish. Americans discovered sushi, the Japanese culinary delicacy made of fish, rice and Asian vegetables. However, as people spend more time in front of their computers and have less need to socialize at lunch with co-workers, a new lifestyle may affect both the health of communities and personal well being.

I Love Sushi: Transforming Bellevue's Culinary History

In 1981, an energetic and imaginative young Japanese man traveled the West Coast from Los Angeles to Vancouver, British Columbia. Yoshi Yokoyama stopped in Seattle and then crossed the floating bridge to Bellevue. "Bellevue was beautiful with the mountains," Yokoyama recalls, and although it still was a small city, "I could feel its energy." He was so taken with the town that he stopped at the City Hall and talked to then Mayor Cary Bozeman. "What can I do for Bellevue?" he asked the Mayor. "You can open its first

Japanese restaurant," replied Bozeman.

That year, Yoshi and his wife, Keiko, leased a former steak house on Main Street and opened Shogun House. When people first visited its sushi bar they admired the art of the sushi but hesitated to eat it, being unfamiliar with the raw fish and rice concept. That changed in the mid-eighties when the medical reports noted the healthy aspects of eating Japanese food and fish, and the movie "Shogun" popularized Japanese culture. Other restaurant chefs, all over America, also began to incorporate Japanese ingredients and culinary technique. Menus offered fusion recipes, combining Eastern and Western cuisines. They also incorporated nouvelle cuisine concepts with small portions on big plates and an emphasis on fresh market foods.[40]

Yokoyama decided to sell Shogun House and open a restaurant that just served fish. He called it I Love Sushi and located in the Midlakes area. Customers at the I Love Sushi bar are fascinated by the display of beautiful seafood and the expertise of the sushi chef who wields a special one-edged Japanese knife to create one complete peel of a whole cucumber. The chef creates a culinary art presentation with rice, fish, avocado, fish roe, wasabi and little sprays of daikon, to give only one example. The art and entertainment aspect of sushi encourages families and friends to come to I Love Sushi for reunions and special occasions.

Yokoyama is passionate about the healthy aspects of fish and the high quality of the food his restaurants serve. Yasuko Nakajima, has worked for the restaurant since 1990. She notes that sushi means in Japanese, "delicious fish" and that 200 years ago, before refrigeration, the Japanese made sushi for special celebrations. They put it in koji, rice with rice wine or sake and soy to help preserve it. Although it appears easy to make sushi, the chef needs training to know what fish to use and must be skilled to maximize the unique combination of flavors and to create the delicate works of art.

Visitors to I Love Sushi can order a variety of small plates including tempura vegetables, tofu made from Vashon Island organic soy milk, delicately marinated and grilled cod, and a calamari salad with ginger dressing, radicchio and baby spinach. To enjoy sushi to the maximum, Nakajima recommends moistening it lightly with soy. Too much soy masks the delicate flavors, she says. Ginger should also be eaten sparingly, preferably between "courses" for the same reason. They serve a special blend green tea, Genmai-cha and Maccha, that complements the Asian flavors.

Yokoyama's newest restaurant, I Love Sushi, on Lake Bellevue, is a co-venture with Chef Masahiko Nakashima. Yokoyama envisions the next stage of his culinary life to reflect Chef Nakashima's expertise in preparing traditional Japanese cuisine. "There is too much fusion now, and it's time to re-introduce authentic Japanese cuisine."[41]

Tested
Black Cod Yuan Yaki
Chef Masahiko Nakashima

4 6-ounce filets black cod
4 ounces sake
4 ounces mirin
4 ounces light soy sauce
0.5 ounces yuzu juice

Marinate cod for 3 hours. Grill.
Yield: 4 Servings

Yonny Yonson and Poppinjay's

 Jack Fecker, one of the partners of the Bellevue Farrell's Ice Cream Parlour, wanted to open a "healthy" sandwich shop. Frogurt, a frozen yogurt dessert, was popular on the East Coast so Yonny Yonson, the name of the new eatery, focused on frozen yogurt, whole wheat breads, cookies made with honey and whole wheat flour. They served no carbonated soft drinks.

With his previous partner in Farrell's, and Bill and Gertrude Popp as investors, Fecker opened Yonny Yonson in 1976 in a small, somewhat hidden shopping center on 148th Avenue NE and NE 24th Street. "Thanks to some incredible radio advertising, it was extremely successful," recalled Popp. The Yonny Yonson experience inspired Popp to open her own café, the first to be located in an "off the beaten path" office park near 520 Highway and 112th Avenue NE. She called it Poppinjay's Café. Catering developed, and soon Poppinjay's was delivering all over the Eastside.

Popp has been in the food business for more than thirty years and has experienced a series of Bellevue food trends. She says that in the 1970's whole wheat foods with no sugar were popular; in the 1980's menus were more balanced with emphasis on smaller portions. In the 1990's people wanted no fat or low fat foods; at the same time, the portions got larger: larger bread slices, larger muffins, bigger cookies. Super-sizing became a new trend.

Popp says, "Today, we are experiencing 'back to healthy.'" Breakfast, not just muffins or pastries, seems to be popular with breakfast sandwiches and protein drinks. We are still in the forefront with fresh sandwich ingredients: quality meats and cheeses, as well as fresh salads, fresh fruit, and fresh pasta salads. Hot entrees are homemade daily. People eat out more and are expecting that the operator be aware of their health needs. We have recently joined the awareness of transfats and how we can diminish their presence in all our foods. . . an awareness of how what we eat affects our ability to function. And, lastly, the most incredible change not directly related to food, is the trend to eat at work, at our desk. We used to experience a room full of happy clients eating and socializing. Our dining room is hardly full while most clients take their food to their desk to eat in front of a computer or talk on the phone. How healthy is that?" Popp asks.[42]

The Bellevue Club: Fitness for Lunch

From swimming lessons to wedding receptions to business meetings, the Bellevue Club serves as an important community center on the Eastside. Members and guests gather in the Polaris Dining Room and in the club's conference areas for informal breakfast and luncheon meetings as well as formal conferences. It is a place where multi-generational families celebrate birthdays and anniversaries. With the opening of a sixty-seven room hotel in 1997, it also offers a get-away destination.

Bellevue Club Polaris Dining Room

The Bellevue Club opened in 1979 with the dual mission to be both a social and athletic facility, an institution known for "wellness, recreation and hospitality." President S.W. 'Bill' Thurston says, "When the club opened there was only one high-rise office building downtown. It's easy to see that Bellevue, a destination city, has come a long way from the bedroom community it was in 1979. . ."[43]

Crossroads: A Market in a Mall

In 1962 Dick Valdez, developer, envisioned the Crossroads Shopping Center as an outside mall and a part of a planned community. In addition to stores, it boasted an ice skating rink and the Red Barn Theatre. By the 1970's it had been enclosed and roofed, but its original sprawling configuration made it difficult to create an identity and loyal clientele.

Ron Sher, managing partner, visited Vancouver's market and hired its architect, Lee Lovelass, to make preliminary drawings for a redevelopment of the Crossroads shopping center as a "market in a mall." In 1986, Microsoft moved to a new campus located in Redmond only a mile from Bellevue's Crossroads area, and other tech companies located in the area. Employees of these new companies came from all over the world, and many settled around the Crossroads area.

Today, food and live music bring everyone together at this Eastside mall, but in the 1970's and early 1980's, the mall risked closure. The Vancouver, Canada, Granville Market inspired a new concept for Crossroads as a gathering place for food and entertainment.

Building on the diversity of the surrounding population, the Crossroads mall established restaurants, totaling seventeen together, that reflected the ethnic backgrounds of these new residents. The management organized comfortable seating areas with tables. The Market Restaurant area seats 900 to 1000 people at a given time. They established and invested in a restaurant service that included using real china and silver for all venues with a trained bussing and dishwashing staff. To help train the many non-English speaking applicants they offered English as a second language class.

With an overall philosophy to be inclusive, they planned diverse programs that attracted people to come to Crossroads to eat and listen to music. Management invested in a main stage with a good sound system and put a sound technician on the payroll. On Friday and Saturday evenings, people come to the Crossroads to eat and listen to a variety of live music presentations, from big band dance style to jazz.

The giant chessboard painted on the mall floor in the north wing attracts players, sometimes speaking in twenty different languages, to play the universally popular game. The Library Connection, a King County Library System branch on the premises, generates a phenomenal circulation and provides computers for users. For the "Bite of Crossroads," held annually, customers buy tickets in order to taste the variety of foods served by the mall food venders.[44]

On the Menu: Late Night in the Market

Bite of India
"Late Night in the Market" attracts crowds to the Crossroads Shopping Center on

Friday and Saturday evenings. Many choose the tantalizing menu at the Bite of India, the creation of Usha Reddy and her husband, Lakshma. They first opened a spice shop and, soon after in 1988, the Bite of India as a part of the Market Restaurants at Crossroads.

The eatery has become a gathering place for Bellevue residents. In addition, Indian families come from Seattle and even from out of state to eat there. More than a thousand customers a week enjoy vegetables samosas; masala dosa, a lentil-rice flour pancake with fillings; sambar, vegetable soup with lentils; and Hyderabad curries, layered casseroles made with vegetables, chicken or lamb served with rice. Usha Reddy believes customers like her cuisine because it is both flavorful and healthy.

Reddy prepares her recipes, spicing them with curry and love. She is passionate about Indian food and cooking it. "I have a recipe for everything. I keep my family style cooking because customers love it. It's like their mother cooking for them." For Reddy, it's not just a business; she has a passion to cook healthy food and to educate customers about it. "There is more joy that way," she says. Many of her recipes have been in her family for generations.

What is the essence of Usha Reddy's South Indian food? "Vegetables are an important component of Indian food. Spices imported from south India are important because in the Indian culture each spice also plays a role in maintaining good health: cumin for digestion and turmeric as a deterrent to disease, for example."

After they opened a restaurant named Golkonda, also located at the Crossroads mall, her culinary talents came to the attention of restaurant critics John Hinterberger, for *The Seattle Times*, and Penny Rawson of the *Journal American*. *The Seattle Times* featured her in its monthly Northwest chef's column, and Reddy is proud that Graham Kerr demonstrated one of her recipes on his televised cooking show.[45]

Tested
Usha Reddy's Vegetable Curry

1 1/2 tablespoons vegetable oil
1 small onion, diced
1 1/2 piece ginger, minced
3 cloves garlic, minced
1/8 teaspoon each turmeric and garam masala
1/2 teaspoon each ground cayenne and coriander
Salt to taste
1/2 cup yogurt
2 medium potatoes, diced
1/2 cup frozen green peas
2 medium tomatoes, cubed
1/2 cup cauliflower, flowerettes

Heat oil in 3-quart sauce pan. Add onions and sauté until golden brown. Add dried spices and yogurt. Cook for 2 minutes. Add vegetables except cauliflower; cook 15-20 minutes. Add cauliflower. Mix well. Reduce heat to low. Cover and cook 5 minutes, stirring occasionally. Serve warm with steamed rice or any of the Indian breads.

Crossroads Farmers Market

In 2006, the Crossroads Shopping Center management decided to create another gathering place for the community and opened its first Farmers Market in the south parking lot. Sixteen vendors brought farm-grown fruits, vegetables and flowers to sell on Tuesdays from May to October. Crossroads partnered with Hopelink to provide volunteers for the information booth and start-up money for the project. The market's success ensures its return in 2007. "Our farmers did well for a first-year market, and we are very pleased," says Susan Benton Crossroads Property Manager.[46]

Hopelink

Food Bank Cooking Classes Demystify American Food Culture

"Why didn't they choose peanut butter?" wondered the Hopelink staff. "How can we help them use the Food Bank?" New Bellevue Residents, often non-English speaking, come to Hopelink for the food bank and other services. Coming from many different cultures and backgrounds, they aren't acquainted with peanut butter and locally-grown vegetables. As a result, Hopelink organized cooking classes and demonstrations to demystify American food culture and to supplement their core services. They deliver services to 7 percent of Bellevue's population..

In 1971, due to massive Boeing layoffs a famous billboard in Seattle asked, "Would the last person leaving Seattle, please turn out the lights!" Local citizens, concerned about growing unemployment, created a community employment service and food bank that grew into a Community Action Agency to alleviate poverty. Known first as the Bothell Multi-Service Center, it soon expanded to locations throughout north and east King County and extended services over the years. When a new facility opened in the year 2000 near 148th Avenue SE and Main Street in Bellevue, the agency adopted the name, Hopelink. The Bellevue Hopelink Center Food Bank serves over 950 families a year. They deliver food to clients who are homebound, disabled and elderly.[47]

A "City in a Park"

As Bellevue Mayor, Nan Campbell, knew that giving public service meant giving up time with families and friends. She says her family understood as long as she kept the family cookie jar filled!

"I have lived in the Bellevue area by Lake Sammamish since 1952, before Bellevue's incorporation in 1953 and before my neighborhood was annexed to Bellevue in 1969. I was elected to Bellevue City Council in 1981 and served eight years, from 1982 to 1989, the last two years as Bellevue's first woman mayor. I came to the Council after the prior City Council had passed the Central Business District Plan that essentially changed Bellevue from a suburb of Seattle into an urban center. During the eight years that I was on the City Council, Bellevue acquired and developed many new park properties and environmentally sensitive areas. I am pleased that the councils that have followed have maintained human services, the environment, and parks as high priorities."[48]

Bellevue Picnics in a Park

Picnic dining was a part of Bellevue's earliest culinary tradition soon after Seattle-ites began to cross Lake Washington by boat or arrived after a drive around the lake, picnic hampers in tow, to enjoy a day in the "country." One of Bellevue's earliest photos shows the William Meydenbauer family enjoying a picnic on their property on

Meydenbauer Bay. Clarissa Colman recorded picnics in her diaries written more than 100 years ago.

Bellevue's early residents packed egg salad or honey and "creamed butter" sandwiches in their picnic baskets; they may have caught a lake fish to fry over a campfire and heated up coffee to drink. In the 1920's, Bellevue's residents enjoyed annual "basket" picnics at Wildwood Park where they participated in races of all kinds, a tug-of-war, and for the ladies a nail driving contest.[49] Prizes included five pounds of butter to the largest family present; a year's subscription to *The Lake Washington Reflector* newspaper for winning a contest; and a slab of bacon to the longest married couple. A 1930's community picnic at Wildwood Park celebrated the new highway connecting Bellevue to Renton.[50]

In 1954, as Bellevue became more urbanized, the Bellevue City Council created a Park Board, realizing the need to provide land for public use. Thanks to their efforts today's Bellevue families and friends can visit sixty-two different parks on a total of 1,711 acres of preserved land.[51] They gather at parks for reunion picnics, bringing along homemade potato and green salads, ham or chicken main dishes, and desserts. They may grill hot dogs and hamburgers. Often, friends meet for concerts and other events held at parks and on lawns where they enjoy a picnic they may have ordered from a caterer. Their box lunch might include any of the following: a vegetable wrap, a roasted veggie foccaccia sandwich or one with deli meat and cheese; salad nicoise, Asian chicken or Caesar salad; for dessert giant cookies, carrot cake, or a brownie; fruit and a bottle of Perrier or wine.

Lee Springgate, Bellevue Parks Director from 1978 to 1999, envisioned that parks should "protect and connect." By acquiring more land, Springgate created a dynamic and interactive system of parks, with connecting trails and green belts. His vision, historically based on Frederick Law Olmsted's concept of parks as "pearls on a string," gave Bellevue its identity as "a city in a park." "Asking me to choose one favorite project over another is much like asking which of your kids you love the best. They are all very special to me. It's hard to decide whether the Downtown Park is more important than, say, Wilburton Hill Park and the Botanical Gardens or the Mercer Slough or Newcastle Beach Park or the Lake Hills Greenbelt or Crossroads Park."[52]

Downtown Park Reception

Marie O'Connell City Clerk from 1982 to 1992 explains the city's growth and the process leading to the development of the Downtown Park.

"It was an extraordinary time in the history of the City's development as a teenage awkward city to an adult thriving city. It was no longer a suburban city to Seattle but a financial and viable city in its own right. It was an era of change, courage and vision and a great deal of work for Council members, staff and citizens. It was indeed a privilege to play a small part in this process. One of the most memorable projects during that time was the acquisition of the land for a Downtown park. The Council wanted a park that was esthetically beautiful, unstructured and quiet.

"*Arc with Four Forms*"
by George Baker,
Downtown Park

The Council had a formal showing of all the design [sic] plans submitted. A public and formal invitation was sent to Bellevue residents to attend a reception and cast their vote for the downtown park design. The event was held at the First Congregational Church. Citizens were asked to view the plans and vote on the plan they liked best.

The staff was in charge of the reception. Everyone had a special fondness for cookies, so they agreed that each contributor would make two batches of their all time favorites. The cookies were served on large silver platters along with a sparkling punch. It was a festive evening and enjoyed by the Council, citizens and staff. Today we have a 'jewel' of a downtown park in the middle of our city thanks to the courageous and thoughtful City Council of that time."[53]

These are like tiny pecan pies - chewy and thick with pecans. Versions of the recipe appear in several popular cookbooks, including The Silver Palate Cookbook.

Tested
Pecan Squares
Marie O'Connell

Crust
2/3 cup confectioners' sugar
2 cups unbleached all-purpose flour
1/2 pound (2 sticks) sweet butter, softened

Preheat over to 350 degrees F.
Grease a 9 by 12 inch baking pan.
Sift sugar and flour together. Cut in butter, using two knives or a pastry blender, until fine crumbs form. Pat crust into prepared baking pan. Bake for 20 minutes; remove from over.

Topping
2/3 cup (approximately 11 tablespoons) melted sweet butter
1/2 cup honey
3 tablespoons heavy cream
1/2 cup brown sugar
3 1/2 cups shelled pecans, coarsely chopped

Mix melted butter, honey, cream and brown sugar together. Stir in pecans, coating them thoroughly. Spread over crust. Return to oven and bake for 25 minutes more. Cool completely before cutting into squares.
Yield: 36 squares

History and Culinary Traditions 1990 to 2000

What's Past is Prologue

The prosperity and development that characterized Bellevue during the last decade of the twentieth century recalls the "Gay Nineties" period of great wealth in New York and Boston at the turn of the nineteenth century.[1] As Bellevue moved imperceptibly towards the twenty-first century, monumental changes to the old order were poised to occur. Development projects threatened historic sites and motivated long time residents to preserve them. New residents wanted to learn about Bellevue since many came from all parts of the world to work on the Eastside, primarily in the new high tech industry. Contributing to aroused community interest in history, a museum of doll art opened, and by the turn of the century the Bellevue Art Museum finally had a home of its own in a new building on Bellevue Way.

What clues did Bellevue's culinary past provide for predicting its future? Volunteers and community leaders remained committed to planning for their community. To organize and plan, they held meetings at new gathering places; the coffee shop became the place of choice for busy people on the "fast track." Over lattes and giant cookies, citizens met to plan the revival of the Strawberry Festival and a heritage center on the Eastside; they undertook the opening of a Botanical Garden and international exchanges. The prosperity during the 1990's made it a heady time and an increasingly global one. The Eastside YMCA hosted international cross-cultural food events, and ethnic restaurants proliferated. The end of the twentieth century heralded in a new era with Millennium fireworks displays and special dinners. Bellevue's past became a prologue for the twenty-first century.

McDowell House, circa 2006

Built in 1918, the McDowell House, located on Wilburton Hill, serves as the Eastside Heritage Center's Administrative offices. The City of Bellevue owns and manages the house, leasing it to the Eastside Heritage Center.

History in Bellevue

Eastside Heritage Center

For decades, Bellevue had been too busy "growing up" and becoming an "Edge City" to find time for its history. By the 1980's, citizens, acknowledging a need for historical preservation, formulated a plan for preserving significant sites, memorabilia and events. In the best Bellevue tradition, founders held their first meeting over cookies and tea in a private home. In 1986, volunteers organized as the Bellevue Historical

Society and fifteen years later, through a merger with Marymoor Museum of Eastside History, became a larger entity called the Eastside Heritage Center.[2]

In 1987, members of the historical society revived the Strawberry Festival, holding the celebration at the Northwest Center on Clyde Hill. Volunteers baked shortcakes and hulled the berries to serve at the event. Lucile McDonald, author of Bellevue's first history book entitled, *Bellevue: Its First 100 Years*, attended as guest of honor.[3]

In 2003, for its sixteenth revival year, the Strawberry Festival returned to its roots in Old Bellevue as a community street fair. That same year, Belle Pastry opened on Main Street, and owner Jean-Claude Ferré graciously allowed Festival volunteers to use his kitchen to store strawberries and baked the Festival shortcakes. By 2006 an estimated 35,000 people attended the two-day event held in the Bellevue Downtown Park on June 24th and 25th, consuming 4,000 pounds of strawberries and 4,500 short-cakes topped with immeasurable amounts of whipped cream.

The Strawberry Festival is the Eastside Heritage Center's signature event, through which it endeavors to create public awareness for the organization and to promote community involvement in and appreciation of Eastside history. Festival participants enjoy fresh strawberry shortcake, entertainment on two stages, historical and agricultural exhibits, family fun with games, clowns, face painting and strawberry shortcake eating contests, food and vendor booths and a classic auto show. A highlight of the Festival each year is an exhibit of working farm equipment from the Kirk Unzelman and Mike Intlekofer Antique Farm Equipment Museum. Also featured at the Festival are berries and flowers produced on two working Bellevue farms, the Mercer Slough Blueberry Farm and the Toulue Cha farm. Beginning in 2007, the Strawberry Festival will be held in Bellevue's Crossroads International Park, making the event more centrally located for participation by the broader Eastside community.

Since 1998, members of the Eastside Association of Fine Arts (EAFA) have donated historical paintings to benefit Bellevue's Strawberry Festival and other Eastside Heritage Center projects. Julie Creighton, the first to participate, painted a watercolor of Bellevue's historic Clyde Hill ferry landing. Creighton's delicious old-fashioned short-cake recipe also takes us back in history. Bake them until they are done, but watch to prevent over-browning.

Tested
Old-Fashioned Strawberry Shortcake
Julie Creighton

2 cups flour
2 tablespoons granulated sugar
1/2 teaspoon salt
1 tablespoon baking powder
1/2 cup unsalted butter, chilled
1 beaten egg
2/3 cup light cream

Preheat oven 450 degrees F.
Sift flour, sugar, salt and baking powder together into a mixing bowl. Cut in the 1/2 cup butter until mixture resembles coarse crumbs.
Mix in the egg and light cream until just blended.
Roll or pat out dough on a floured surface to 1/4 inch thickness.
Cut into 3-inch circles with a cookie cutter.
Bake shortcakes on a greased or parchment-lined cookie sheet for about 10 minutes or until lightly browned.

Split and place each one on a plate. Spoon cleaned and sliced strawberries over the shortcake and top with whipped cream. Garnish plate with one whole perfect berry.
Yield 6 shortcakes

Bellevue Historical Society

Founders of the Bellevue Historical Society held their first meeting over cookies and tea in the home of Margot Blacker. Margot served eight years on the Bellevue Planning Commission and on the Bellevue City Council from 1990 to 1998.

Tested
Dream Cake or Slice
Margot Blacker
"...this is so rich and good." Everyone wants this recipe, so here it is!

Pastry
1 cup of flour
1/2 cup of butter

Preheat oven to 350 degrees.
Mix well and spread on bottom of a 9" x 9" pan. Bake while you are mixing the topping until pastry browns a little - about 15 minutes.

Filling
2 eggs
1cup of brown sugar
1 teaspoon baking powder
1/2 cup of shredded coconut
1 teaspoon vanilla
1 cup chopped walnuts

Reduce oven temperature to 325 degrees F.
Combine filling ingredients. Pour over the 'pastry' bottom. Bake until topping sets and browns, about 30 minutes

Cool and ice with a butter icing which is a mixture of softened butter and powdered sugar and a little cream and vanilla. Mix to a desired consistency and spread on cooled slice. Cut into squares and arrange on a plate.

The Winters House Kitchen

In 1989, the City of Bellevue acquired the Winters House, located on Bellevue Way next to the Mercer Slough Park, and it became the first house in Bellevue to be placed on the National Register of Historic Places. After a two-year restoration effort, the Winters House reopened in 1994, and visitors who tour the 1920's era house learn about its Spanish architecture and its unique tile floors and decoration. The 1920's kitchen has period appliances: a Westinghouse Automatic Flavor Zone Oven Junior console range circa 1928 and a General Electric refrigerator circa 1930 with a foot pedal to open the door. According to the *Historic Structure Report*, "The kitchen and breakfast nook floor finish tile is laid in a basket weave pattern of light green rectangular tile and small square dark green tiles. The border around each room is a black band of small square tiles in a regular grid pattern."[4] Kitchen items of interest include a Ball pressure cooker, Fiesta dinnerware and Depression cut-glass ware, a vintage Fisher flour sack, an antique toaster, historic tins and food containers and old advertisements.

After a two-year restoration effort, the Winters house reopened in 1994, and with the assistance of Eastside Heritage Center docents, visitors who tour the 1920's era house learn about one of Bellevue's historic sites.

Dolls and Tea Parties

Winters House Heritage Tea

In August 2002, Heather Trescases, with a Masters of Arts in Public History, moved

Special Guests Winters House Heritage Tea

to Bellevue from Toronto, Canada. She began volunteering for the Eastside Heritage Center (EHC), first as archives and research assistant and co-coordinator of the 2004 Strawberry Festival. Since she became Executive Director of EHC in 2005, she has encouraged new programs, including a historic bus tour and the mini-museum exhibitions in downtown Bellevue, and exhibits at the Bellevue Farmers Market, in the Bellevue Arts Museum café, the Fraser Cabin and the Bellevue City Hall. At

the Winters House Heritage Tea, a new event in 2006, guests enjoy tea and touring the Winters House historic rooms. By attending the heritage tea to be with friends and enjoy the refreshments, participants give support to the preservation of Bellevue's history and create a new Bellevue culinary tradition.

Winters House circa 1929

Heritage Tea Menu

Fruit Platter

Scones

Cucumber and Cream Cheese Sandwiches

Raspberry, Apricot and Lemon Tarts

Rosalie Whyel Museum for Antique Dolls and Tea Parties

The visitor enters the Rosalie Whyel Museum of Doll Art to discover a world of dolls, some from another age; many from different cultures. The museum has world-class status and is located in a Victorian style building on the southeast corner of NE 12th Street and 108th NE. Its collection displays over 1500 dolls, dating from 1680 to the present. The displays describe the dolls' provenance and their social and cultural contexts. The museum exhibits also include toys, bears and miniatures. The museum is

German Wooden Doll, 1820 – 1840 and Antique Kitchen

a popular venue for birthday parties, weddings and tea parties held in the Rose Room and English Garden.[5]

Doll Museum English Tea Party* Menu

Tea Sandwiches (tuna, egg salad or cheese)

Fresh Seasonal Fruit

Mini Raspberry or Key Lime Tarts

Raspberry Tea

*The English Tea Party is served on an elegant china tea service.

Bellevue Botanical Garden Tea Parties

"A nation would be better off without gold than to be short of trees," quotes Anna Littlewood, former Bellevue Botanical Garden Board member. Littlewood calls the botanical garden a shelter that is a "daily changing palette of color and texture" serving as a wild life habitat with fifteen varieties of birds. "Winterscape sparkles with the low hanging sun backlighting trees and the frost beaded spider webs. . ."[6]

Bellevue Botanical Garden

In the 1980's, Bellevue established itself as a "City in a Park" with green spaces and outdoor venues for picnics, activities and sports. According to Iris Jewett, "Then, things began to line up" for Bellevue to have a Botanical Garden. Iris and others dreamed of a Botanical garden that would be a repository for plant conservation and where visitors could view well-documented plant collections.[7]

In 1984, Calhoun and Harriett Shorts deeded their Wilburton home and surrounding seven acres of gardens to Bellevue. The City Council, Mayor Nan Campbell, the Parks Department, directed by Lee Springgate, and the Parks Board, headed by Margaret Miller were all receptive to the idea of a botanical garden located on Wilburton Hill.[8] To gain public support, Iris helped organize public meetings and the concept gained acceptance, although it would take eight years for the garden to become a reality. When the thirty-six acre garden opened in 1992, Iris said, "I was thankful, but I didn't know if anyone would come!"

The Shorts' former home serves as the visitor center where people hear lectures, take classes and see exhibits. Over the years, culinary-related demonstrations have included a Cooking with Herbs class, a Chinese New Year celebration with fortune cookies and an all-day event on how to use seaweed, coconut and chocolate to create Chocolate Sushi. The Botanical Garden hosts an annual garden tea on Mothers Day. In the early years, when founder Cal Shorts attended, they always had a cup of coffee ready for him.

Meetings over a Cup of Coffee

Bellevue volunteers traditionally have accomplished a lot over a cup of coffee. The coffee revolution made it a lot easier. Starbucks Coffee, originating in 1971 in Seattle, spawned and spread the Northwest coffee revolution across America and overseas.[9] Howard Schulz's efficient espresso bars on street corners, in department stores and office buildings, offered a welcome alternative to stale coffee on a hot plate in the office lunch room or having to spend time in a restaurant for a lunch, when only a cup of coffee is required. Quick, inexpensive, and accessible, coffee shops transformed social interaction; heads of corporations sit at tables doing business next to students working on laptop computers.

Tully's Coffee Shops: A Place to "Sit and Sip"

A resident of the Bellevue area where he lives with his wife Cathy and their three children, Tom "Tully" O'Keefe founded Tully's Coffee in 1992, giving his middle name to the company. Although it sounds Irish, it was actually passed down from his Uncle Tully of Greece.

Today, more than 350 Tully's operate in the Western United States, with other outlets in Japan. Tully's prides itself on its specialty coffees roasted in small batches and the inviting atmosphere of their shops. According to a Tully's spokesperson, their shops offer "comfortable furnishings where everyone can find a place to 'sit and sip,' conduct informal meetings, get wrapped up in a good book, laugh with a dear friend, make progress on some pressing assignment without distractions, sketch, people watch, let the kids play with toys found in the store box, read the newspaper or just relax."

Tully's supports community projects by donating coffee for walking and touring events, in the Wetherill Nature Preserve, for example, and by participating in fund-raising for children's and welfare organizations. Tully's partners with local manufacturers, the Wilcox Dairy, among others, in their support of the local community.[10]

Bellevue's Grand Central Bakery

In 1989, Gwenyth Bassetti, with Alan Black, purchased the bakery in Seattle that became known as the Grand Central Bakery. Bassetti was the first to introduce "artisan" breads to the Northwest. In 1994, Bassetti crossed the bridge to Bellevue to attend an auction. After 38 years, Arthur's Bakery closed, and Arthur Wilk was selling an antique box-tying machine and two old baker's tables that Bassetti wanted to purchase. She bought them, but when she learned that Bellevue would no longer have any downtown bakery, she proposed to her partner Alan Black that they lease the old bakery building between NE Second and Main Street from the Wilk family and open a second site for the Grand Central Bakery. They remodeled the bakery to display their artisan breads and pastries, installed a French-made oven, redesigned the interior and set up tables outdoors where customers enjoyed the sunny days. Friends and business acquaintances who frequented the bakery regretted the closing in the late 1990's.[11]

Tested
Giant Oatmeal Chocolate Chip Cookie
Grand Central Bakery

For a "chewy in the middle, crisp on the edges" cookie be sure to make these in the large format as described. The two kinds of chocolate chips produce a very tasty, slightly sweet cookie.

1/2 pound (two sticks) unsalted butter, room temperature
1 cup granulated sugar
1 cup brown sugar, lightly packed
2 large eggs
1 1/8 teaspoon vanilla extract
2 1/4 cups all purpose flour
1/4 teaspoon salt
1 1/8 teaspoon baking soda
1 1/8 teaspoon baking powder
2 1/2 cups oatmeal
1 cup semi-sweet chocolate chips
1/2 cup milk chocolate chips

Preheat oven to 350 degrees F.
Cream butter, sugar and brown sugar in mixing bowl until very light in color and fluffy (approximately 6-8 minutes). Scrape bowl well. Beat in one egg at a time, beating until fully incorporated. Scrape bowl well. Add in vanilla and beat until incorporated. Measure together flour, salt, baking powder and baking soda. Set aside.

Measure together oats and both types of chocolate chips. Set aside.
Add flour mixture all at once to butter mixture and mix until just combined and no
traces of flour remain making sure to scrape down sides of bowl.
Add oats and chocolate chips, mixing gently until just combined.
Using a levered ice cream scoop (or a large spoon) drop cookies on a parchment lined
baking sheet with 2 to 3 inch spacing between each cookie.

Gently press each cookie to flatten slightly.
Bake until cookies are slightly golden (approximately 15-20 minutes). Rotate pans
halfway through baking if necessary for evenness.
Remove from oven and transfer to racks to cool.
Cookies should be slightly crisp around the edges and slightly chewy in the center.
Yield: (16) large cookies

Bevan Bellevue Jewelers Hosts a Wedding

Although stores often have grand openings with food to introduce customers to their business and products, Bevan Bellevue Jewelers became the first Bellevue business to host a wedding. The Bevan family opened its jeweler business in 1954 in Bellevue Square, across from the theater. "My brother Gail and I were so fortunate in our timing and in the location," said Norris Bevan of their decision.[12]

Bevan Bellevue Jewelers
Hosts A Wedding

In 1991, Gail Bevan's daughter, Linda Bevan-Wyatt, and her cousin, Phil Bevan, started their own jeweler business, locating it in Bellevue Place and calling it Bellevue Jewelers. In 1992, Phil and Linda illustrated their family's sense of community when they offered the Bellevue Place store as the site for a wedding. A young man who made frequent deliveries to Bellevue Place, and his fiancée wanted to marry but suitable sites were difficult to find at the price they could afford. The Bevans offered their store. They moved back the jewelry cases and set up chairs, ordered a cake and champagne, and City Flowers supplied flowers for the hour-long service.[13]

Phil and Linda hosted another celebration in 2004 when they moved the business to Main Street. Three hundred longtime friends and loyal customers attended the opening celebration. With wedding cake and receptions, the Bevan family created community ties.

Food and Culture

Culinary Links Create Cultural Bridges

The act of "breaking bread" together creates and sustains relationships. With food comes understanding. One bite and cultures reveal themselves and their roots: Hot corn on the cob, dripping with butter? A Midwest American farm tradition for dinner. Corn ground into flour, made into dough and fried? A Mexican tortilla. Powdered ginger combined with molasses, eggs, sugar and flour ingredients with decorated icing? A German Christmas cookie. Fresh ginger pickled and served with fish and rice wrapped in seaweed? Japanese sushi. Each food reveals food sources, geographical location and traditions. Since the 1980's, Bellevue's restaurants represent many cultures and many dining styles. Each one cited here represents a piece of Bellevue's culinary history, adding to the telling of its story.

La Cocina del Puerco

Authentic, different, casual with funky metal chairs, Bellevue's version of a Mexican cantina describes La Cocina del Puerco located on Main Street. "We're fighting the Rodeo Drive trend on Main Street," laughed owner Bill Baker. His wife, Pat Baker, with Greg Gahner and Blair Boand, opened the restaurant in 1985, but in 2001, Pat and husband Bill took full ownership.

Born in Mexico City, Pat's fluency in Spanish proves invaluable working with menus, recipes and a staff of eight, some of whom have Spanish as their first language. The modest restaurant serves Mexico City style, including homemade tamales with chunks of roasted pork or tomato sauce on chicken and taquitos de carne asada with grilled flank steak. Pat uses her family's recipes, and her mother makes the salsa fresh daily. Her sister Liz is manager. Their recipes use no lard, no sour cream, no melted cheese and only corn oil. They also make their guacamole fresh every day.[14]

Workers and shoppers come in for lunch; apartment and condo dwellers drop in for supper, for take-out or to meet friends. The name of the restaurant means "Kitchen of the Pig," but this family-operated restaurant, perhaps more correctly, could be called La Cocina de la Familia, The Family Kitchen. Olé...

Burnt Cream
Pat Baker

2 cups whipping cream
8 egg yolks
1 cup sugar
2 tablespoons vanilla extract

Preheat oven to 375 degrees F.
Mix and pour into 12 to 14 oven-proof ramekins. Place ramekins in a baking pan in a hot water "bath." Put the pan of ramekins in the oven and bake 1 hour. Remove when they are set and sprinkle with cinnamon. Chill before serving.
Yield: 12 to 14 servings

Dixie's BBQ: Slow Cooking and Lively Laughter

Perhaps the most unusual Bellevue culinary story is almost hidden, beside a con-

crete support for the 520 highway running above Northup Way. The first-time visitor searches to find the
famed eatery located in a former auto-repair shop.
The search is well worth it, because homemade bar-
becue awaits, succulent, spicy and just downright good. Customers may have to wait
in the line that frequently forms to get into Dixie's, and Gene Porter, the owner, may
be directing traffic when you pull into the parking lot. "It's worth the wait," said one
customer who, although not normally a fan of barbecue, admitted that the tender,
moist chicken, perfectly napped with a piquant freshly made sauce, tasted wonderful.

Word of mouth has made this one of Bellevue's most popular lunch venues. A lot
of well-known citizens have eaten Dixie's barbecue, including Microsoft's Bill Gates
and former Congresswoman Jennifer Dunn. "We are very down to earth around here,"
says daughter, LJ Porter, "so when you come here, construction workers and attor-
neys, family members and doctors all take a minute out of their day to just sit and have
a good time. Laughter is a great healer for the soul."[15]

Gene Porter's father came to Seattle in 1963. Gene and his wife, Dixie, followed,
opening an auto-repair shop in Bellevue. In 1970, they bought a home in the Newcastle area. The family moved from New Orleans, but Dixie had roots in North Carolina
and Gene in Mississippi. Dixie brought her family recipes to the Northwest. The family began to prepare their BBQ meals for weekend church benefits. Gene kept a pot of
barbecue going in his auto-repair garage. Over the years, they perfected the recipes,
and people who had the good fortune to taste them encouraged Gene and Dixie to start
a business selling their celebrated barbecue.

In 1994, they converted the auto-repair garage into a restaurant. After only two
weeks of opening, the word got out, and a newspaper article featured them. "From
serving 80 people a week we jumped to serving 800 after that article," recalled LJ. Her
brother, known as "Porter," operates a catering business, Porter's Place. The family
also sells the barbecue at Safeco Field.

"Slow cooking is a big part of it,' says their daughter, LJ Porter, best known as one
of the top rhythm and blues singers in the Northwest. They use quality meats and
marinate the ribs before grilling and smoking them. The most popular meals at Dixie's
include the pork and beef sandwiches with side dishes of red beans and rice, potato
salad, cornbread, lemon cake, baked beans, pasta salad or sweet potato pie.[16]

Then, there is "The Man." Gene Porter brings to customers' tables a potent pan of
barbecue sauce, known as "The Man," and it is transforming. One patron fond of spicy
food asked for a serving. Just one bite and he took off his coat, reached for a cold glass
of water and said "Wow!"

Dixie's transports its customers to another world of food. The Porters are justly proud, not only of their success, but also that they can make people happy and bring them together by the simple act of cooking.

YMCA Cross-Cultural Cooking Classes and Picnics

In the 1960's, the East-side YMCA opened its doors at 14230 Bellevue-Redmond Road, responding to the growth of population on the east side of Lake Washington. Since opening, the Eastside YMCA invested in many programs to promote community building.[17]

YMCA Kobe Exchange, 1960's

The Greater Seattle YMCA initiated a joint-venture project in the 1960's that included the YMCA of Greater Seattle, the Eastside YMCA and the Kobe, Japan, YMCA and began exchanges between the two countries. In 1992, the Eastside YMCA offered a cross cultural program designed to help Japanese families moving to the Eastside for three to five year stays because of jobs in the developing tech industry. Because of the language barrier, Japanese wives were more isolated than their husbands. Masako Yamamoto began offering cooking classes, flower arranging and picnics to help the women and their families adjust to their new lives in Bellevue. Three hundred Japanese women enrolled in the cooking and culture classes. Offered as a cross-cultural program, the classes also taught Japanese culinary traditions. As a feature of the program, participants celebrated Japan's Tanabata Festival, sampling traditional Japanese noodle and chicken dishes. The Japanese women also wanted to know more about American recipes, in particular how to bake fruit pies, a delicious way to learn about Bellevue's berry heritage.[18]

Heritage Recipe
"Steamed Chicken with Pickled Plums"
Mariko Miyake

2 chicken breasts
3 or 4 umeboshi (pickled plums)
1/2 cup tororo kombu (shredded and flavored dried kelp)
2 tablespoon sake (Japanese rice wine)
Pinch of thin-sliced ao-shiso (green shiso leaves)

Cut each chicken breast in half lengthwise, then cut thin slices diagonally.
Sprinkle on sake and marinate for a few minutes. Spread chicken evenly on microwave
dish. Remove pits from umeboshi and tear into pieces and add to the chicken. Cover

dish and microwave on HIGH for 6 to 7 minutes. Discard the drippings and cool for a
few minutes. Sprinkle tororo kombu and eat with ao-shiso.
Yield: 4 servings

This specialty recipe can be used as an accompaniment to the main dish in a Japanese meal...Tei-shoku. Because of the specialty ingredients, this may be challenging for the home cook to attempt. Mariko Miyake, was one of a number of key volunteers who demonstrated this recipe to participants.

Bellevue Sister Cities Association

Sister cities build friendship, trust, trade and understanding through people-to-people exchanges. Bellevue's sister city links stretch to Yao in Japan, Hualien in Taiwan,

Liepaja in Latvia, and Kladno, in the Czech Republic. Bellevue and Liepaja became sister cities in 1992, a year after Latvia gained its independence following the break up of the Soviet Union. Dr. Zaiga Phillips, a Latvian-born Bellevue pediatrician, led the efforts to join the two cities in order to encourage student and teacher exchanges and to contribute medical supplies for Liepaja hospitals, books and computers for their schools.

Located opposite Sweden on the eastern shore of the Baltic Sea, Latvia has had numerous invaders and occupiers, all bringing their own traditional foods. As a result, Latvia's culture is rich with culinary traditions including a biscotti-like cookie; a saffron "kringel,"

Bellevue Sister
City Hualien,
Taiwan, Statue

or large pretzel baked for birthday celebrations; and piragi, a popular appetizer.[19]

Tested
Pumpernikli (Latvian-style Biscotti)
Mirijama Karlsons

3 eggs
1 1/2 cups granulated sugar
3/4 cup raisins or currants
3/4 cup hazelnuts or almonds, chopped
1 teaspoon baking powder
2 cups all-purpose flour

Preheat oven to 350 degrees F.
Combine the eggs and sugar. In a separate bowl mix the flour and baking powder.
Stir the sugar mixture into the flour with a spoon and with your hands if necessary,
incorporating the fruit and nuts. Refrigerate for an hour.
Flour your hands and roll dough into 4 long ropes, about 17 "long. Brush the tops with
egg.

Place rolls on two 12.5 inch x 17.5 inch baking pans lined with parchment or with a Silpat(r), silicone, sheet. Bake in a preheated oven about 20 to 25 minutes until light brown. Remove baked rolls from the pan to a cutting board, cool slightly and cut diagonally into 1/2 inch slices. Bake again for about 10 minutes on each side. Cookies should be dry and crispy. Cool on racks. Cookies will keep for several weeks in tightly sealed tins.
Yield: 5.5 dozen

These cookies have a sweet, nutty flavor. With cranberries instead of raisins they look pretty as Christmas gifts. They also could be dipped in chocolate. Good served with a cup of coffee, hot chocolate or a glass of sherry.

Tribute to the Bellevue Larry's Market

The Bellevue Larry's Market retains a special place in Bellevue's culinary history. Larry's offered fresh, local farm-to-market products and prepared foods before the idea became popular. Larry's always retained family ownership and a smaller retail concept. One of six in a chain of Larry's stores, the Bellevue Larry's Market opened in 1991 in the Midlakes district south of NE 8th Street; its lunch room and deli items made it especially popular at noontime.

"If you need it, you can find it at Larry's. Need ideas for your party or reception, the knowledge of our associates is excellent and many are chef trained. If you need a special cake, we can do it, and with real French butter cream," said Mark McKinney, company spokesman, in a 2006 interview. Larry's catered the Bevan Bellevue Jewelers' Main Street store opening. Unfortunately, the Bellevue Larry's Market closed its doors in September, 2006.[20]

The Meydenbauer Center
Community Banquets and Receptions

City leaders decided that Bellevue had the population, economic base and the business potential to merit its own convention center. Built in 1993, the Meydenbauer Center serves as a center both for the community and for commercial interests. The community gathers there for banquets and receptions to recognize citizens for the Best of Bellevue, Advance Bellevue, Youthlink Community Leadership Awards, Bellevue Chamber of Commerce events and for Bellevue Downtown Association annual dinner and community awards.

The Meydenbauer Center

Other events at the Meydenbauer Center are fundraisers, including the Bellevue Schools Foundation "Spring for Schools" Luncheon, the Overlake Hospital Auxiliaries'

Bandage Ball, the YWCA Annual Benefit Luncheon, the Overlake Service League "Step Up to the Plate" Benefit Luncheon, the Hopelink "Reaching Out-Rebuilding Dreams" Luncheon and the Youth Eastside Services Luncheon. For community gatherings and events, food plays an important part in the success of all these events.[21]

Celebrating the Millennium: Year 2000

The Millennium evoked a range of responses, from doomsayers predicting an apocalypse to romantic idealists conjuring fantasy dreams for the twenty-first century. In between lay the majority, calmer and more pragmatic about stepping into the new century. Bellevue celebrants commemorated the event, some on a grand scale with fireworks. In response to the growing interest in natural and local foods, others chose a dinner that would be significant for the twenty-first century, and for such a special occasion dined at The Herbfarm Restaurant in Woodinville. The Herbfarm Restaurant provides fine cuisine with an emphasis on the use of herbs. Chef Jerry Traunfeld has gained acclaim for his fine cuisine and the dining experience at The Herbfarm Restaurant. For dinner on December 31, 1999, he planned a special Millennium menu for his guests to enjoy as they awaited the arrival of the new century.[22]

The Herbfarm
New Year's Eve
DECEMBER 31, 1999 – JANUARY 1.

Your Dreams, O Years,
How they penetrate
through me!

WALT WHITMAN.

A MENU FOR
The Last Supper
OF THE TWENTIETH CENTURY
AT THE HERBFARM
FRIDAY, DECEMBER 31, 1999 · 7.30 O'CLOCK

Beginnings of the End
Quail Egg Benedict
Pacific Spot Prawn in Wild Matsutake Mushroom Broth
Gravlax Salmon Tart
Half-Shell Olympia Oysters with Tuberous Nasturtium
CHAMPAGNE: 1985 KRUG, LATE DISGORGED

Three Caviars
1990 VEUVE CLICQUOT LA GRAND DAME BRUT

Oregon White Truffle and Celery Root Ravioli
1961 CHATEAU MARGAUX PAVILLON BLANC

Souffle of Dungeness Crab
With Chervil and a Sea Urchin Sauce
1994 FRITZ HAAG BRAUNEBERGER JUFFER-SONNENUHR AUSELESE

Seared Duck Foie Gras
With French Lentils and Stuffed Prunes, Glazed Shallots
Sauce Madeira
1900 BARBEITO MALVAZIA MADEIRA

Squab with French Black Truffles
Wrapped in Savoy Cabbage with Leeks
1994 BROADLEY VINEYARDS PINOT NOIR,
CLAUDIA'S CHOICE

Dom Perignon Martini
With a Lemon Geranium and Rosemary Olive

Crusted Saddle of Fallow Venison with Oregon Black Truffles
Fingerling Potatoes, Bloomsdale Spinach,
Thumbelina Carrots
1982 CHATEAU MOUTON-ROTHSCHILD

Roquefort & d'Yquems
Roquefort Cheese with Roasted Quince, Dried Cherry and Apricot Chutney, Winter Greens and Thyme Cracker
1975 CHATEAU D'YQUEM SAUTERNES
1983 CHATEAU D'YQUEM SAUTERNES

Auld Lang Syne: End of the Century
1989 PERRIER-JOUËT FLEUR DE CHAMPAGNE ROSÉ

Stilton, Pear, and Pair of Ports
Pear Tart with Stilton Cheese Crust and Spiced Walnuts
1963 FONSECA PORT
PRE-PHYLOXERA 1880's PORTO ROCHA 'MILLENNIUM' PORT

Golden Star and Silver Moon
Scharffen Berger Chocolate Cake
and Hazelnut Praline Ice Cream
with Caramelized Satsumas

Brewed Coffees, Teas & Infusions

A Selection of Small Treats
VINTAGE 1795 BARBEITO TERRANTEZ MADEIRA

With Food Comes Understanding: 2000 to 2007

After the Millennium, construction projects of epic proportions changed Bellevue's downtown landscape, while an increasingly diverse population infused the city with vitality and ingenuity.

Believing in Berries

Bellevue's abundant resources drew pioneers to its shores; its rich land sustained them. Early settlers harvested Bellevue's abundant berries. Sweet and juicy, berries became a renewable resource thanks to the efforts of diligent farmers.

Bellevue's twenty-first century volunteers and leaders must sustain resources that address more complex problems than the cultivation of berries: children, schools, the arts, and the preservation of history. To give one example, the community recognized that some Bellevue school children came to school without breakfast and did not have money for a hot lunch. Several Bellevue organizations now give support and donate food to help meet this problem.

The universality of food creates an opportunity and a solution. Bellevue's citizens joining together to solve problems follow the tradition set by those who organized the original 1930's hot lunch program, baked shortcakes for the Strawberry Festival, raffled blueberry pies for Chamber of Commerce benefits, sold ice cream bars for Rotary at the Arts and Crafts Fair, baked cookies for a community reception to review Downtown Park designs and attended benefits for Overlake Hospital.

In the 1940's, internment shattered the lives of Bellevue's Japanese citizens. Today, sister city organizations, cross-cultural food programs at the YMCA, student language class exchanges, the availability of ethnic restaurants and specialty shops, restaurateurs who sponsor charitable events, all contribute, in the environment of food, to improved awareness. Food informs understanding of other cultures and ways of living.

The "New" Old Main Street

Bellevue's culinary history comes full circle and ends where it began, on Main Street. Today modern condominiums rise above the thoroughfare that in the early 1900's carried horses, wagons, and Model-T's. A reprise of Main Street's original old McKee building façade embellishes the shop fronts where Fran's Chocolates and other enterprises reside below a new modern condominium. But for the decades the center of downtown was several blocks north, the old

City of Paris Building
on Main Street, 2006

landmarks live on in the new restoration.

Main Street in the twenty-first century certainly can claim to be the one authentic piece of heritage real estate where pedestrians can stroll along a street of historical memories. The City of Paris building at 104th Avenue NE and Main still stands, a reminder of when community leaders sat at Meta Burrows' Lakeside Drug soda fountain to plan for the community. South of Main Street near 102nd Avenue NE stands Mrs. Carter's Boarding House, currently an antique shop. At the east end, at the intersection of Bellevue Way and Main Street, a new development will replace the historic Russell barber shop and Toy's Café. Fortunately, these two longstanding businesses remain on Main Street at new locations.

Main Street has regained its original importance for shoppers who used to come there for provisions at McGauvran's and Streams' Groceries and for Green River sodas at Meta Burrows' soda fountain. Twenty-first century customers shop at Porcella's European Market and the Zizo Mediterranean Market and eat at the many restaurants now available.

50 Fest: Bellevue's Yearlong Birthday Party

At the time of its incorporation as a third class city in 1953, Bellevue was home to 5,940 residents. Fifty years later, in 2003, Bellevue's population was 117,000.[1] In 2002, the Eastside Heritage Center invited community leaders to form a planning committee for a yearlong celebration to commemorate Bellevue's fifty years of incorporation. Walt Crowley, Alan J. Stein and the HistoryLink staff published the *Bellevue Timeline* to showcase Bellevue's history. The Bellevue City Council supported the celebration plan and dedicated $100,000 to help underwrite its costs. For the commemoration, to be known as 50 Fest, the committee planned a year long series to promote public appreciation of Bellevue's history and to engage all of Bellevue, its neighborhoods and community representatives, in an "exploration of the city's past, present and future."[2]

To involve as many citizens as possible in the celebration, the committee planned many events, including neighborhood parties, picnics, a history treasure hunt and a 1950's-style Sock Hop. To kick off the year of celebration, they gave a party at the Meydenbauer Center. Bellevue's four Sister City mayors and spouses attended the celebration.[3]

Four hundred people attended the official 50 Fest Birthday Party, including many past and present dignitaries. In addition, Bellevue neighborhoods celebrated with their own birthday parties.

50 Fest Birthday Party Menu
March 31, 2003

Spinach and Cheese Phyllo Pastries
Focaccia Gorgonzola Triangles
Goat Cheese Profiteroles with Caramelized Shallots
Crab Stuffed Tomatillos
Chicken Satay Skewer
Tomato Basil and Feta Toasts

Reminiscences: Former Mayor Connie Marshall

"I am only the second woman to have the honor to be Mayor in 52 years. It was a HUGE honor to be Mayor during our birthday year. . . The 50 fest was the RIGHT year at just the RIGHT time. Our community was in the midst of a significant downturn in the economy and, I believe, everyone was so ready for a party! We had a GREAT community 'team' of people who did all the planning and organizing. John Valaas, CEO First Mutual Bank, and I raised the money - difficult time to raise money, but a great cause, so the companies generously gave us the funds.

The community had a GREAT time. There were larger community events: Initial Celebration - which was the formal event and we hosted all four of our Sister Cities - Sock Hop at BCC, traveling time line, community parties: Factoria, Lake Hills and Crossroads Shopping Center.

We thought there would be about a half dozen neighborhood birthday parties - turns out over seventy neighborhoods celebrated their own birthday parties!! The culmination event was the Fourth of July Fireworks. . . a grand celebration."[4]

The Changing Urban Scene in Downtown Bellevue

Speaking before those gathered for lunch at the Women's University Club March 30, 2006, Kemper Freeman, Jr., son of the founder of Bellevue Square, described Bellevue's vital economy and energy. He reminisced about Bellevue in 1946 when Bellevue Square opened with sixteen stores and Bellevue had no hospital, to the current time with the new Lincoln Square project.[5] Lincoln Square, across from Bellevue Square in the downtown core of the city, adds to the complex of skyscrapers decorating Bellevue's skyline. Freeways to the east, south and north and a network of wide avenues crowded with cars crisscross Bellevue passing new construction sites that erase familiar landmarks. The automobile has defined Bellevue since the opening of two bridges crossing Lake Washington from Seattle. Now, new downtown development projects will allow residents to live within walking distance of the library, post office, art museum, shopping and restaurants.[6]

Grand Opening Events for The Westin Bellevue

The Westin Bellevue Hotel anchors Lincoln Square, a center with retail stores, restaurants, a 16-screen movie theatre and twenty-three floors of condominiums. November 1, 2005, three hundred guests attended the grand opening event that included entertainment by the Tuxedo Junction big band and professional ballroom dancers from the Bellevue Arthur Murray dance studio. Kemper Freeman, Jr. gave a welcoming address, as did hotel General Manager, Matt Van Der Peet.[7] The cocktail reception offered Orange Wasabi Shrimp, Duck Breast with Wild Berry Compote, Mini Lamb and Veal Chops and other gourmet specialties. A three-course dinner followed.

Bellevue Westin Grand Opening
Three-Course Plated Dinner

Salad
Ahi Tuna Tartare, Avocado and Ogo Salad, Lemon Scented Olive Oil

Entrée
Pan Seared Beef Tenderloin, Roasted Forest Mushrooms on
Mascarpone Herbed Polenta

Desserts
Lemon Citrus Cake, Passion Fruit & Raspberry Sauce, White Chocolate Garnish
Dark Chocolate Dome, Caramel, Crème Fraîche, Dark Chocolate Garnish

Performing Arts Center Eastside
PACE Candlelight Dinner and Art Auction

PACE, or Performing Arts Center Eastside, came into being in 2003 to establish

a performing arts center with a theater that would accommodate an audience of two thousand to attend musicals, opera, the Bellevue Philharmonic and other events. Suzanne Hutchinson organized a guild of forty women to act strictly as a fundraising arm of PACE. The guild presented its first fundraising event in 2004, an art auction and candlelight dinner, held in the Bellevue Wintergarden. After a cocktail reception and silent auction, four hundred diners enjoyed the following menu and participated in the live auction to help raise money to fund a Main Stage Grand Piano, a 9-foot Steinway Concert

PACE Dinner-Auction
Item, 2006

Grand, being built in New York. The auction and dinner became an annual event. In 2006, Northwest artists decorated life-size statues of reindeer, "bucks." Different businesses and institutions sponsored and displayed the colorful statues all over the downtown and on Main Street for several months before the auction. The Candlelight Dinner and Buck Auction on October 21, 2006 raised $525,500.[8]

The Candlelight Dinner & Buck Auction
2006 Benefit Menu

During the Cocktail Reception
Bruschetta
Crab Cake with Garlic Aioli Sauce
Herbed Goat Cheese Tartlet with Roasted Red Pepper Salsa
Phyllo Pastry with Feta, Spinach & Oven Roasted Tomato with Cucumber Yogurt
Dinner
Soup
Butternut Squash
Salad
Baby Arugula & Field Greens, Roasted Bosc Pear, Sundried Cranberries,
Stilton Blue Cheese and Toasted Walnuts with Sherry Vinaigrette

Entrée
Grilled Beef Tenderloin and Tiger Shrimp, Gratin Potato, Green Asparagus &
Roasted Plum Tomato with Marsala White Truffle Reduction

Wine
Chateau Ste. Michelle, Columbia Valley Pinot Gris
Chateau Ste. Michelle, Columbia Valley Syrah

Dessert
Lemon Tear Drop with Trio Coulis

"Gather. Celebrate. Innovate." Bellevue's New City Hall

"Gather! Celebrate! Innovate!" These words echo the dynamic of community effort to plan and innovate. Opening ceremonies for Bellevue's City Hall on May 20, 2006, commemorated those efforts. Mayor Grant Degginger and City Council members spoke of the twenty-year vision and commitment that led to building the new structure, nine stories high with state-of-the-art technology.

Bellevue City Hall

The new City Hall will serve the community both for official business and private events: weddings, concerts, and programs inside and out on its new plaza and park.[9]

Thirty-five hundred citizens came to celebrate under blue skies and spring sunshine. They gathered around the plaza and along the wide walkway leading to the spacious entrance of their new City Hall. In a tribute to Bellevue's diverse heritage and sister city connections, Chinese lion dancers and Japanese Taiko drummers heralded the opening ceremony before officials cut the symbolic red ribbon allowing visitors to enter. Upon entering City Hall, they passed by historic photos of Bellevue and descended to the first floor where City Catering Company served individual Triple Chocolate Chiffon Cakes topped with Dark Chocolate Ganache and Orange Chiffon Cakes frosted with Orange French Buttercream.[10]

Seventh Biennial Sculpture Exhibition Reception

A reception held June 17, 2006, in Bellevue's newly inaugurated City Hall celebrated the opening of Bellevue's Biennial Sculpture Exhibit and honored the artists. "We had fifteen sculptures on display, outside on the plaza, along the second level walkway and in the main concourse. Mayor Grant Degginger and Arts Commission Chair, Roxanne Shepherd, welcomed the crowd of artists and fans of the exhibition. The weather was beautiful, and after the opening events celebration at City Hall many people continued the celebration by going to the Downtown Park to see the additional nineteen sculptures there," said Mary Pat Byrne, Arts Specialist for the City of Bellevue since 1987.[11]

Historic Washington State Dinner: The Gates' Cake

Bellevue's new landscape may symbolize its sky-high economic aspirations, but a dinner gave it a place in the region's international history. On April 18, 2006, in the late afternoon, helicopters flew over Bellevue anticipating the arrival of China's President Hu Jintao for a Washington "State" dinner, not in Washington, D.C., but at Bill and Melinda Gates' home in Medina, Washington. Governor Christine Gregoire, other state officials and business leaders attended the dinner to meet the guest of honor, China's President Hu Jintao on his first official visit to the United States. The purpose of the dinner was to build trade relations.[12]

The Gates' Dinner Menu

First Course
Smoked guinea fowl salad with Northwest hazelnuts, spring radishes and Granny Smith apples

Entrées
Filet of beef with Walla Walla onions, local asparagus and a celeriac purée
and chervil glacé
Served with a 2002 Leonetti Cellars Cabernet Sauvignon
or
Alaskan halibut and spot prawns with spring vegetables, fingerling potatoes
and smoked tomato infused olive oil
Served with a 2003 Chateau Ste. Michelle Chardonnay, Canoe Ridge Estate.

Dessert
Brown Butter Almond Cake

The Gates' Cake

Perhaps one of the more unusual stories of Sherry Grindeland's journalistic career at *The Seattle Times* Eastside Bureau came from researching the recipe for the Gates' cake. Readers wanted to know how to bake the cake served to China's President Hu.

Grindeland baked the cake and commented about it in her column published April 18, 2006. ". . . The Cake isn't difficult. Just allow yourself time to brown the butter, chop the rhubarb and separate the eggs. Browning the butter requires constant attention. If you let it go just a few seconds beyond brown and a nutty odor, you'll have burned and stinky. And be forewarned that browned butter shrinks in the process. Start with about pound of butter to get the 6 ounces. Jue suggests that home cooks bake the cake in a loaf pan, like banana bread. I doubled the recipe and baked it in a 10-inch springform pan (like a cheesecake) because I wanted the drama of the round cake and some left over to share with family." Because the Chinese delegation requested no dairy products, the Gates served the cake plain. Grindeland recommends serving it with whipped cream.[13]

Tested
The Gates' Rhubarb Brown Butter Almond Cake
From pastry chef David Jue

3/4 pound butter (to reduce to 6 ounces)
1 cup almond flour
1 2/3 cup powdered sugar
1/2 cup all-purpose flour
5 1/3 ounces egg whites (5 large eggs)
1 pound rhubarb, chopped into 1/4 inch pieces
A little apricot jam, melted and brushed on as a glaze

Preheat oven to 375 degrees F.
Brown the butter. Sherry: "Stay close to the stove while it is browning. It burns easily. You want it golden brown. Strain it and discard the solids left in the pan and strainer. Let

the butter cool, but don't let it harden."
Sift the dry ingredients together. Add the dry ingredients to the egg whites, mixing well.
Fold in the brown butter. Refrigerate at least one hour or as long as a week.

Chef David Jue used individual ring molds to bake the cakes for the presidential din-
ner, pouring 1/2 cup batter into each mold. Sprinkle about two ounces or 1/2 cup of
the finely chopped rhubarb pieces on top. Lightly push them into the batter. Bake in a
preheated oven for 10 to 15 minutes, until light brown. Jue suggests home cooks bake
the cake in a loaf pan, like banana bread. If you choose that option, expect it to take 30
minutes to bake.
Let rest. When cool, brush lightly with a glaze made of melted apricot jam.
Yield: 6 servings

Bellevue's Food Revolution

The "Dining Out" section of the April, 1978, *Bellevue Spectrum* looked back to the 1954 restaurant scene and noted the following: "While Bellevue Square was coming into being, Bob Minkler bought the Village Inn, Walter Clark opened Clark's Crabapple (acquired from Carl Pefley), and Dave Cohn started The Barb. Four miles away, Dave and Jim Born, brothers and partners took over the Flame in Kirkland. . ." The article described them all as "family-style restaurants."[14]

Fifty-three years later, Bellevue's restaurants exist in downtown Bellevue, in Factoria, in Lake Hills, at the Crossroads Shopping Center and in numerous small shopping areas around the city. The variety astounds, from ordering off a Northwest local catch menu and being served in a fine dining room on a white linen tablecloth to calling out an order at a Taco Truck parked near NE 8th Street and 156th Avenue NE. Supermarkets and specialty stores also sell prepared foods for lunch and dinner, appealing to "families on the go" as an alternative to fast food chains.

Bellevue families like to eat out and might choose to go to the Red Robin in the Bellevue Square Mall; Burgermaster, the popular 1967 Drive-In near Highway 520; the Azteca on 112th Avenue NE; California Pizza on 106th Avenue NE or to Chantenee, a Thai restaurant near Main Street. High school students find a quick, inexpensive lunch at Chipotle's off NE 4th and at the various locations for Subway and Quizno's.

More recently Bellevue residents can buy their food from farmers markets and favor organic and natural foods. To connect with the old ways, to remember the flavors of "real" food, perhaps that provides the consistency of the familiar everyone needs while so much change occurs around them.[15]

The Bellevue Farmers Market

On June 17, 2004, Lori Taylor opened the Bellevue Farmers Market in a church parking lot near NE 17th Street and Bellevue Way. Fittingly, she chose the same location that John Clarke had cleared in the 1920's to cultivate grapes. She revitalized Bellevue's most enduring legacy from its founding days as an agricultural community and, at the same time, created a means for improving community life and relations. Taylor grew up in Bellevue, but spent her summers on her grandparents' Wisconsin farm. "Farming is in my genes, and it just seemed to me that Bellevue should have its own farmers market."[16]

She sees the market as a great community event that serves and benefits many. "The pur-

Bellevue Farmers Market

pose is to provide small family farms in our state a viable place to sell their crops directly to the consumer and to give the community a gathering place that is festive, fun and beneficial."[16] For the 2006 market, forty-eight vendors came with their produce, cheese, meat, honey, flowers, fish, baked goods and more. At the end of each market day, farmers have the opportunity to give leftover produce to Hopelink, the local food bank. Last year, Hopelink received over 7,000 pounds of fresh produce for their clients valued at over $10,000. "Music, chef demos, non-profit booths, the market is like a town square, and in this day and age it is great to see people from all walks of life getting together and experiencing community," Taylor says enthusiastically.

Vendors, who offer colorful displays of fruits and vegetables picked when ripe and often of an unusual variety, include the Hedlin Family Farm in La Connor, Martin Orchards in Orondo, Ellensburg's Kittitas Valley Greenhouse, and Willie Green's Organic Farm in Monroe. The Golden Glen Creamery in Bow, Washington, sells artisan cheeses; Fishing Vessel St. Jude, troll catches and cans its own tuna; Taylor Shellfish offers mussels and clams. Also for sale are artisan breads, eggs, mushrooms, nutmeats, and herbs. Hmong growers add color to the market with their beautiful flower displays.[16]

Pierce Milholland painted the Hmong and immigrant farmers for the 2004, 2005 and 2006 posters used to advertise the market. Milholland leaves a lasting tribute to the immigrant worker he depicts in his vivid paintings. His art hangs in private homes, local banks and hospitals. He died in 2005, and Lori Taylor sees his art as a constant reminder of the debt we owe to farmers and the land.

Rain City Cooking School: "Everyone has to eat."

In 2001, Carol Dearth opened a cooking school in Bellevue. "As a Navy wife of 26 years, I have spent a good deal of time moving around the globe. When my husband took orders to Naples, Italy, I fell in love with the food there. So, I learned to cook it. And then my friends began to ask me to teach them what I had learned. My college degree is in adult education, so I began teaching Italian cooking, and a career

was born." Improving cooking skills is important, she believes, because "everyone has to eat."[17]

As for food and culinary trends, "I think the culinary arts are evolving, with more varieties of foods available to us each and every year, and more information about cooking. Food TV has developed a tremendous amount of interest in food and cooking. On the flip side, people are not learning the basics of cooking anymore. We are not teaching it in many of the schools, and few young people are learning it at home - they are eating take-out. Those who are truly interested are seeking out cooking schools.[18]

Organic foods are changing the way we shop for food for our families, and will ultimately change the way food is produced as the demand grows. We need to be educated in what this means as a consumer - does organic mean better, or just more expensive? What are the benefits, how is it a good thing for us as a consumer?"[19]

Dearth goes on to say, "I am attaching a recipe for stuffed zucchini blossoms that I learned to make in Naples. Each time I make these, it takes me back 20 years to my time there, the wonderful food, the warm, friendly people. Italian food is always about what is at the peak of the season, and how to best showcase the fresh unique flavors of that food. It is my favorite cuisine."[19]

Look for Dearth and her students at the Bellevue Farmers Market where they sometimes shop for food they all cook together later that day in class. Zucchini blossoms are available at the Bellevue Farmers Market.

Tested
Stuffed Zucchini Blossoms
Chef Carol Dearth

12 zucchini blossoms
1/2 pound ricotta
1 egg
salt and pepper
1/4 cup freshly grated Parmesan
olive oil, for frying
flour for dredging

Preheat oven to 170 degrees F. Gently wash and dry zucchini blossoms, taking care not to tear the delicate flowers. Pat dry with paper towels. Trim stems to 1-inch. Mash ricotta with fork, add eggs, salt, pepper, and Parmesan, mix well. Using a small spoon or a pastry bag, carefully fill blossoms half full. Fold ends to close. Dredge in seasoned flour, and shake off excess.

Heat 3/4 to 1 inch of olive oil in large skillet, to 350 degrees F. Gently lower stuffed blossoms, a few at a time, into hot oil. Turn gently to cook to golden brown on all sides. Remove to paper towel lined tray. Keep warm in 170 degree F oven. Serve warm.

Bellevue Whole Foods Market

Gourmet and natural foods joined forces when John Mackay opened his first Whole Foods Market in Austin, Texas. The Bellevue store opened at NE 8th Street and 116th Avenue NE in 2004, selling natural and organic products.. As more Americans have concerns about food "miles," food sources and food production, Whole Foods turns to local market products and local producers. In the summer of 2006, Whole Foods invited local farmers to hold a Farmers Market on their property. Only the farmers participated in the profits. The store plans to invite farmers once a month during the summer of 2007. The Bellevue store sells berries grown by the Mercer Slough Blueberry Farm and is helping the blueberry farm create a label for its frozen berries.

With a wide variety of gourmet cooked-to-order and prepared items, the Whole Foods Market becomes for many a take-out restaurant and deli. Whole Foods hosts Community Support Days, with 5% of the day's profits going to community and non-profit organizations. They partner with organizations like The Bellevue Schools Foundation, Bellevue City Parks and the Eastside Domestic Violence Program. The Overlake Service League was a recent recipient of a donation.[20]

Whole Foods "Salud!" Sunday Family Dinners

"... I have had a lot of really good feedback and positive reaction to my 'Sunday Family Dinners' series. This is a format in which everyone in attendance gathers around a communal or 'family' table and gets to share a meal, meet each other, and learn a bit about who lives in the area. I give them recipes and demonstrate my cooking techniques as everybody relaxes and enjoys a glass of wine or other beverage. I think our Bellevue customers are learning about a lot of new foods, and we have a very exciting milieu of ethnic backgrounds shopping here," Chef J.J. Johnson.[21]

Koots Green Tea: Lattés with an Asian Twist

Koots Green Tea, the Japanese green tea retailer with café outlets, opened its flagship U.S. store May, 2006, in Bellevue's Lincoln Square complex. Founder, Kouta Matsuda, created green tea specialty drinks as an alternative to specialty coffee beverages. He wanted to update the traditionally formal Japanese tea culture to encourage interest again in green tea, declining in popularity especially among young Japanese. Matcha, used for centuries in the Japanese Tea Ceremony, currently enjoys popularity as a nutritious beverage "rich in antioxidants, minerals, vitamins, fiber and amino acids."[22]

To create his matcha lattes, Matsuda conducted experiments with an espresso machine, using green tea powder. In the beginning, his drinks exploded, but after many trials and modifications of the espresso machine, he successfully made the smooth, subtle tasting matcha latte that launched his new business.[23]

Because of his father's international business, Kouta Matsuda grew up all over the world, in Africa, Europe and the U.S. While going to high school in the U.S., friends gave him the nickname, "Koots." Hence, the name for the tea business that he created. For ten years, his company operated Tully's Coffee Japan, building the chain to 300 outlets.

Matsuda knew that many Americans wanted an alternative to coffee, and that they appreciated the healthy attributes of green tea. He also saw food as a cultural bridge after experiencing the reactions to the Japanese lunches he brought to school when a schoolboy in Africa. He envisioned the tea business in a global context. He opened the first Koots Green Tea shops in Japan in 2002.

According to a February 2007 interview with store manager, Tatsuo Tomeoka, Seattle is considered the "specialty drink capital of the world." Matsuda believed that a new drink concept would appeal to a sophisticated clientele. Matsuda chose Bellevue for his flagship U.S. store because he could see the potential for growth in Bellevue. January, 2007, a second Koots opened in Seattle at 2200 Westlake near the new Whole Foods, a good location for Koots since they emphasize their certified organic teas. The health benefits of green tea and the atmosphere of the cafés appeal to those who are "on the go" and have their matcha latte in a take-out paper cup as well as to those who appreciate the Japanese cultural experience of drinking tea while sitting in the straw-matted tatami room, spending time with friends or contemplatively enjoying quiet moments drinking tea.[24]

Main Street: Neighborhood Food Connections

From the 1920's to mid-1940's, Main Street had most of Bellevue's business. That changed with the development of Bellevue Square and outlying areas of Bellevue. As a result, in the 1980's and into the 1990's, some Main Street stores closed for lack of business. The 2007 look of Main Street belies the contention held in those days that Main Street would not survive, that it would be ruined by development, and that all its former charm would be erased.

Belle Pastry Shop

Born in Normandy, France, Jean-Claude Ferré began his career as an apprentice pâtissier at the age of 14. In 2002, he opened the Belle Pastry shop on Bellevue's Main Street. He has created it in the style of French bakery and pastry shops. Visitors enter the shop through French doors, greeted by the aroma of freshly baked baguettes and a tempting array of pastries: croissants, miniature fruit tarts, Napoleons and chocolate éclairs. Tables and chairs line windows looking onto Main Street and a parking square. A bouquet of fresh roses sits on a round table in front of a wall-size French art print. Belle Pastry opened the same year the Strawberry

Festival returned to Old Bellevue. Ferré graciously allowed festival volunteers to use his kitchen to store strawberries and baked the festival shortcakes.[25]

Belle Pastry Shop

Fran's Chocolates: A Community Connection

Fran Bigelow first learned cooking techniques with Julia Child's instructive *Mastering the Art of French Cooking* books in the 1970's. She especially loved the challenges of making pastry and creating desserts that "demanded complete perfection." Attending a pastry program at the California Culinary Academy, she studied under European pastry chefs who convinced her to pursue her passion.[26] Fran's Chocolates, a fine confection recognized world-wide, succeeded partly because people had already begun to care about specialty foods, but primarily because of Fran, herself, and her special background, culinary abilities and creative skills.

As a child growing up in Seattle, Fran Bigelow learned about chocolate from her grandmother who often took her to visit chocolate shops from Seattle to Vancouver. Her grandmother knew good chocolate and taught Fran to be meticulous when assessing it. In her book, *Pure Chocolate*, Fran also lists among inspirations for her own creations Frederick & Nelson's Victorian creams and personalized Easter eggs. The influence of the Mounds bar that Fran loved as a child is found in the Fran's coconut Gold Bar.[27]

Fran's Chocolates Shop on Main Street

Fran Bigelow's passion for chocolate is similar to that of a fine wine maker. Attend one of her seminars to learn about different kinds of chocolate, its origins and manufacture, how to cook it and store it, and what to serve with it. Attendees also discover the pure flavor of exceptionally fine chocolate, henceforth finding it difficult to accept anything less.

In 1998, Fran's Chocolates opened its first shop in Bellevue and, in 2004, moved to its present location on Main Street. Inventive, as well as artistic, Fran has created chocolate-covered apricots and figs, many expressions of the popular truffle, salt-topped caramels and chocolates topped with a soupcon of gold or lavender cornflower. Soufi Farzanehpour, Bellevue store manager, and Rosita Fong give knowledgeable, friendly information and encourage the visitor to linger and admire the festively boxed candies. In fact, Fran Bigelow sees chocolate and its community connection as fundamental. She says that she feels the responsibility of "making everyone's special moments stellar."[28]

Bis on Main

Bis on Main opened in 1998, the brainchild of Joe Vilardi and Michel Fredj who

Bis Dining Room

envisioned a restaurant with white linen on the tables and service for lunch and dinner. The two men began in Bellevue by purchasing and operating Fortnum's, a tea and lunchroom located near the intersection of 104th Avenue NE and Main Street. This was the same location that had been a mecca for Main Street business and community leaders for forty years when Meta Burrows' Lakeside Drug and soda fountain operated.

The two owners soon transformed the tea shop and changed to new hours that attracted a broader customer base. When Joe Vilardi became sole owner, he redefined the menu with "Continental and New American" cuisine. Today, Chef Christopher Peterson, with experience at several venues, including La Campagne in the Pike's Street Market, creates tasty dishes using Northwest products from local distributors: Essential Bakery, Paradise Gourmet and Corfini Gourmet, among others. Vilardi believes that dining out should be entertaining, as with a guest who comes to dinner at home. In addition to the meal itself, the restaurant décor contributes to the dining experience. Rotating colorful paintings by Northwest artists decorate the restaurant's walls.

The restaurant remodeled and reopened October 17, 2006, with a new bar and two dining rooms. The neighborhood bar and restaurant concept has increased appeal as Bellevue becomes more urbanized and daily exchanges more impersonal.[29]

Thanksgiving at the Seastar Restaurant

In 2002, John Howie's entrance onto the restaurant scene came at the right culi-

Chef John Howie
Seastar Restaurant

nary moment for Bellevue. The townspeople "seemed to be waiting" for a good seafood restaurant to open in Bellevue and have been enthusiastic about the food and wines Howie serves at his Seastar Restaurant and Raw Bar. His seafood and small plates prepared with wide-ranging flavors please customers, whether they are young professionals who work downtown or retirees relocating to Bellevue's new high rises. "I've worked with a lot of different world cuisines and since the world is primarily water almost all of those cuisines have a great seafood-based component to work with. I love what the different cultures do with raw foods: Japanese sushi and sashimi, Hawaiian po-ke, South American, Central American, Caribbean and Spanish style civiche and seviches, French style seafood tartars as well as local oysters and other chilled seafoods. I wanted a place where people felt comfortable coming in and snacking on smaller portions and could enjoy a varied and wide ranging culinary experience."

The story of John Howie is more than an account of his successes as a chef, because he serves more than seafood; he also serves the community. Each year since he opened in 2002, Howie hosts, donates and participates in approximately twenty-six major charitable events. He gives out more than $35,000 a year in gift certificates alone to local schools and charitable organizations. He hosts the Bellevue Muscular Dystrophy Lock Up event that brings in about $100,000 annually. Howie's son was diagnosed at age five with muscular dystrophy. Howie served as host Chef for the March of Dimes Celebrity Chef Event and supports Children's Hospital.

Thanksgiving at the Seastar adds a complement to Bellevue's culinary story. Howie and his wife decided that Thanksgiving was a day to give back to the community. By partnering with the Overlake Service League, Hopelink and Olive Crest, Seastar hosts a dinner for low income families who come to the restaurant and enjoy a four course meal. Some of Seastar's purveyors donate products as well. John Howie's commitment recalls Bellevue's early efforts that linked food with community projects.[30]

Conclusion
Food as a Cultural Bridge to Globalization

Food provides a clue to contemporary Bellevue's complex and diverse lifestyle: strawberries, specialty coffees, cookies, gourmet chocolates, seafood, market-to-table produce, organic and natural foods, ethnic cuisines, Washington wines and, more recently, green tea lattes. These foods have changed restaurant menus and supermarkets and often people's understanding and appreciation, whether for one of the world's cuisines or for a new Bellevue resident born in India, Japan or Mexico. Indeed, for Bellevue, the world has become "flat" as a result of globalization in the twenty-first century.

For the past one hundred years, community events and celebrations provided good food and conviviality and transformed Bellevue, the rural town, into the urban center it is today. What next? People look for continuity, for the familiar. The past helps them imagine the future and comforts those fearful of change. The common thread, the one that provides constancy and stability, is the connection with food and, especially, the traditions food engenders. Connections and traditions bring everyone to the table to give, share, plan and dream together. For Bellevue, the beautiful red strawberry, so important at the beginning of this story reappears as a fitting ending and hopeful predictor of the future.

In 2003, an eighth grader, Brynn Watanabe, wrote a winning essay for the Strawberry Festival Essay Contest. Her words nicely sum up the meaning and the tradition of food in Bellevue.

Strawberry Festival Essay

"What Do Strawberries, Japanese Americans and Diversity Have to Do with Bellevue"

By Brynn Watanabe

"If you think about it, strawberries are a lot like people. When you first look at them they generally look the same, but when you take a closer look you see each strawberry is different and unique in its own way. And when you put them together they are good. With people it's the same, we're all the same just look a little different and when you put us together, we can mix well, with great results!"[31]

Appendix One: Culinary Timeline

Bellevue Culinary Timeline

1886 Clarissa Colman's Diaries and Pioneer Food
1904 Sakutaro Takami: First Recorded Strawberry Field
1908 McGauvran's Main Street Mercantile
        The Grubstake Grocery Boat
1911 Fruit and Flower Mission
1918 *The Lake Washington Reflector* and LeHuquet Extracts
1924 Hennig's Grape Juice
1925 Strawberry Festival
1929 Summit Winery
1930 McDowell Candy Shop
1931 Younger's Mints on Main Street
1933 Bellevue Vegetable Growers Association
        Sydnor's Blueberries
1934 Meta Burrows' Lakeside Drug and Soda Fountain
1936 Bellevue School Lunch Program
1944 Lakeside Supermarket
1946 Bellevue Square Opening
        Crabapple Restaurant
1947 First Arts and Crafts Fair
1951 Bellevue Blueberry Festival
1954 Kandy Kane Kafe Hospital Benefits
1955 Kingen's Drive-In
        Bellevue Boy's Club Teen Canteen
1956 Arthur's Bakery
        First Quality Food Center (QFC)
1958 Pancake Corral
        Toy's Café
1960 Overlake Hospital Grand Opening
1975 Cooking Classes "Chez Nancy"
1977 Yankee Kitchen Shop
1979 Paul Thomas Winery
1983 Downtown Park Design Community Reception
1984 Bravo Pagliaccio
1987 Strawberry Festival Revival
1988 Crossroads Market in a Mall

1992 Tully's Coffee

      Eastside YMCA Cross-Cultural Cooking Classes

1993 Meydenbauer Center

2000 Millennium Celebrations

2002 Belle Pastry Shop

      Seastar Restaurant

2003 Bellevue 50 Fest

      Performing Arts Center Eastside (PACE) Benefits

2004 Bellevue Farmers Market

      Fran's Chocolates on Main Street

2005 Westin Hotel Grand Opening

2006 Gates' Washington State Dinner for China's President Hu Jintao

      New City Hall Opening Reception

Appendix Two: Recipes

Appendix Three: Reviewers and Evaluators

Text Reviewers
Claypool, Terry
Hart, Donna
Intlekofer, Mike
Knauss, Tom
LeWarne, Charles
Piro, Mary Ellen
Sandbo, Patricia
Trescases, Heather
Williams, Jacqueline
Williams, Barb

Recipe Evaluators
Adams, Laura
Alton, Arlene
Anderson, Sue
Balint, Lyn
Beeftink, Carol
Collins, Carolyn
Danz, Margie
Dickman, Gaby
Forest, Joan
Fujii, Emily
Gopinath, Rama
LeWarne, Anne
LeWarne, Pauline
Lewison, Mary
Newcomb, Arielle
Pederson, Wanda
Sandbo, Patricia
Sherk, Lynn
Walsh, Maro
Weir, Kristi
Wilcox, Margaret
Williams, Steve
Wolgemuth, Joan

Appendix Four: Photos and Images

Photo Credits
Eastside Heritage Center (EHC) unless otherwise noted. Collections from EHC unless otherwise noted.

Front Cover
William Meydenbauer Family Picnic. Meydenbauer Collection. Original Watercolor, Julie Creighton.

Back Cover
"Strawberries." Original Watercolor, Julie Creighton.

Strawberries and Early Community Life 1869 to 1940
1. *Puget Sound Native American Fish Cookery.* Courtesy Hancock Publications. Pen and Ink Drawing Julie Creighton.
2. *Cooking Stove Flue Scraper, circa 1925.* Photo Credit, Steffen Fanger
3. *Mrs. Carter's Tea Room, circa 1930.*
4. *Wildwood Pavilion, circa 1910.*
5. *Grubstake Grocery Boat, circa 1910.* MOHAI (Museum of History and Industry, Seattle, WA) Collection.
6. *Medina General Store, circa 1920.* John Frost Collection.
7. *Fisher Mills Recipe Pamphlet, circa 1923.*
8. *Joe's Place Advertisement, circa 1930.*
9. *Mickleson Family Making Cider, circa 1935.*
10. *Pre-World War II Bellevue Farm Map.*
11. *Strawberry Airmail Stamp, 1938.*
12. *Strawberry Festival, circa 1930.*
13. *Sydnor's Blueberry Label and Recipes, circa 1935.* Rhoda Sydnor Collins Collection.
14. *Fruit & Flower Mission, circa 1911.*
15. *Hill Family Children's Tea Party, circa 1919.* Phyllis Hill Fenwick Collection.
16. *Bellevue Clubhouse.* Strawberry Festival, Japanese Girls in Kimono.
17. *Jane McDowell Candy Shop interior, circa 1930.* Diana Schafer Ford Collection.
18. *World War II Sugar Rationing Coupon.* Diana Schafer Ford Collection.
19. *Jane McDowell Candy Shop exterior, circa 1930.* Courtesy Marguerite Schafer Eminson.
20. *Younger's Mints, circa 1931.*
21. *Main Street, circa 1930.*

22. *Meta Burrows' Soda Fountain, circa 1940.* Meta Burrows Collection.
23. *Marguerite Groves' Recipe Box, circa 1930.* Courtesy Patricia Sandbo. Photo Credit, Steffen Fanger
24. *The Lake Washington Reflector.*
25. Avertisement from *The Lake Washington Reflector.*
26. *Eugene W. LeHuquet.* Sylvia LeHuquet Wilson Collection.
27. *LeHuquet Extract Vehicle.* Courtesy Robere Le Huquet.

Food for Gracious Living 1940 to 1970

1. *Carl Pefley and Duncan Hines Award.* Pefley Collection.
2. *Crabapple Restaurant interior, circa 1947.* Courtesy Annie Stevenson. Florence Christiansen, standing.
3. *Kandy Kane Kafe, Carol Barber and Bellevue Citizens, circa 1960.*
4. *Pancake Corral.* Courtesy Pancake Corral.
5. *Arthur's Bakery: Elaine Wilk Decorates Bellevue Square Celebration Cake 1981.* Courtesy Wilk Family.
6. *Freeman Fire Engine Caroling Party, circa 1960.* Courtesy Freeman Enterprises.
7. *Bellevue Frederick & Nelson Tea Room.* MOHAI, Frederick & Nelson Collection
8. *Bellevue Frederick & Nelson Candy Counter, circa 1950.* MOHAI, Frederick & Nelson Collection.
9. *Frango's Box, circa 1950.* Photo Credit, Steffen Fanger
10. *Lakeside Supermarket: left to right Tina Rudulph, Lucile Birdseye, Gladys Burnell and Myrtle Carr Burnell, circa 1944.* Photo Credit, Bill Brant.
11. *Pacific Northwest Arts and Crafts Fair, circa 1950.* Courtesy Bellevue Arts Museum.
12. *Blueberry Festival: "Princess and blueberries . . .," circa 1957.* Greater Bellevue Washington.
13. *Overlake Blueberry Label, circa 1947.*
14. *Bellevue Arts Museum Arts and Crafts Fair, 2006.* Courtesy Bellevue Arts Museum.
15. *Bellevue Boy's Club Teen Canteen 1955.* Greater Bellevue Washington.
16. *Village Vittles Cookbook, circa 1950.* Craig Hook Collection.
17. *Meydenbauer Bay Yacht Club.* Courtesy Meydenbauer Yacht Club.
18. *Overlake Golf & Country Club Benefit Dessert.* Courtesy Overlake Golf & Country Club.
19. *Belle-View Brand Vegetable Label, circa 1940.*
20. *Overlake Service League Breaktime-Mealtime.* Courtesy Overlake Service League.

21. *Antique Lunch Box, circa 1920.* Courtesy Evalyn Summers. Photo Credit, Steffen Fanger

22. *Toy's Café.* Photo Credit, A.J. Harding.

23. *Burgermaster Drive-In.* Photo Credit, Thomas Knauss.

Diversifying Food Traditions 1970 to 1990

1. *Julia Child 1971 Frederick & Nelson Demonstration.* MOHAI, Frederick & Nelson Collection.

2. *Yankee Kitchen Logo.* Courtesy Nancy Lazara.

3. *"The Yankee Kitchen Almanac and Cooking School Gazette" Fall, 1983.* Courtesy Nancy Lazara.

4. *Mr. J's Culinary Essentials Logo.* Courtesy Debbie Jaffe.

5. *Mr. J's Culinary Essentials Kitchen Shop.* Courtesy Debbie Jaffe.

6. *Junior League of Seattle.* Courtesy Junior League of Seattle.

7. *Frederick & Nelson Sundae.* MOHAI, Frederick & Nelson Collection.

8. *Marvel Morgan, circa 1969.* Preuss Collection.

9. *Hennig's Grapes.* Hennig Collection.

10. *Hennig's Grape Juice Label, circa 1920.* Hennig Collection.

11. *Paul Thomas Dry Bartlett Pear Wine, circa 1980.* Courtesy Paul Thomas.

12. *Bravo Paggliaccio Pizza Chef, circa 1980.* Courtesy Dorene Centioli McTigue.

13. *Cavatappi Wine Label.* Courtesy Peter Dow.

14. *Bellevue DeLaurenti Store.* Courtesy DeLaurenti Family.

15. *DeLaurenti Advertisement.* Courtesy DeLaurenti Family.

16. *Napoleon Co. Logo.* Courtesy the Napoleon Co.

17. *Liebchen Delicatessan.* Courtesy Lynne Rosenthal.

18. *Bellevue Uwajimaya Logo.* Courtesy Uwajimaya.

19. *I Love Sushi Logo.* Courtesy I Love Sushi.

20. *Poppinjay's Logo.* Courtesy Gertrude Popp.

21. *Bellevue Club Polaris Dining Room.* Courtesy Bellevue Club.

22. *Bite of India.* Courtesy Usha Reddy.

23. *"Arc with Four Forms" by George Baker, Downtown Park.* Photo Credit, Thomas Knauss.

History and Culinary Traditions 1990 to 2000

1. *McDowell House, circa 2006.*

2. *Special Guests Winters House Heritage Tea.*

3. *Frederick and Cecilia Winters House, circa 1929.*

4. *German Wooden Doll, 1820 - 1840 and Antique Kitchen.* Courtesy Rosalie Whyel Museum of Doll Art. *From The Rose Unfolds: Rarities of the Rosalie Whyel Museum of Doll Art* by Rosalie Whyel and Susan Hedrick, 1996.

5. *Bellevue Botanical Garden.* Courtesy Bellevue Botanical Garden.
6. *Tully's Logo.* Courtesy Tully's.
7. *Bevan Bellevue Jewelers Hosts A Wedding.* Courtesy Bevan Family.
8. *Cocina del Puerco.* Photo Credit, Thomas Knauss.
9. *Dixie's BBQ.* Photo Credit, Thomas Knauss.
10. *YMCA Kobe Exchange, 1960's.* Courtesy Seattle YMCA.
11. *Bellevue Sister City Hualien, Taiwan, Statue.* Photo Credit, Thomas Knauss.
12. *The Meydenbauer Center.* Courtesy Meydenbauer Center.
13. *The Herbfarm Restaurant Menu.* Courtesy The Herbfarm Restaurant.

With Food Comes Understanding 2000 to 2007

1. *City of Paris Building on Main Street, 2006.* Photo Credit, Thomas Knauss.
2. *50 Fest Logo.*
3. *Bellevue Westin Grand Opening 2005.* Courtesy Bellevue Westin.
4. *PACE Dinner-Auction, 2006.* Courtesy Suzanne Hutchinson.
5. *Bellevue City Hall.* Photo Credit, Thomas Knauss.
6. *Bellevue Farmers Market Logo.* Courtesy Lori Taylor.
7. *Bellevue Farmers Market.* Courtesy Lori Taylor.
8. *Rain City Cooking School.* Courtesy Carol Dearth.
9. *Koots Green Tea Logo.* Courtesy Koots Green Tea.
10. *Belle Pastry Shop.* Photo Credit, Thomas Knauss.
11. *Fran's Chocolates Logo.* Courtesy Fran's Chocolates.
12. *Fran's Chocolates Shop on Main Street.* Courtesy Fran's Chocolates.
13. *Bis on Main.* Courtesy Joe Vilardi.
14. *Chef John Howie Seastar Restaurant.* Courtesy John Howie.
15. *Strawberries.* Original Watercolor, Julie Creighton.

Endnotes

Strawberries and Early Community Life 1869 to 1940

1. Stein and the HistoryLink Staff, *Bellevue Timeline,* 16. Karolevitz, *Kemper Freeman, Sr. and the Bellevue Story,* (1984), 3.

2. Jay Wells, "Celebrating 90 Years since the Lowering of Lake Washington." Presentation at the Winters House, (2006).

3. McDonald, *Bellevue,* 38.

4. Batdorf, *Northwest Native Harvest,* 25.

5. Orchid, *Christina's Cookbook,* 58, 144.

6. Sherry Grindeland, "1800's diary tells of murder mystery, life on Eastside," *The Seattle Times,* Eastside Edition, August 5, 2006.

7. Williams, *The Way We Ate,* (1996), 123.

8. Clarissa Colman, "The Colman Diaries, 1886 - 1916," Eastside Heritage Center Archives. Sherry Grindeland correspondence 23 February 2007. ". . . She [Clarissa] never mentions receiving money for lunches. . . . Then there's also the question of what she means by lunch. In Midwest farm area, lunch means what we'd call coffee break fare - coffee and cookies or cake or light sandwiches." <http://www.HistoryLink.org>, Essay 5045, Foss Tugboat history refers to "Naptha-fueled" vessels. Naptha is familiarly known as camp fuel, or white gas.

9. McDonald, *Bellevue,* 38.

10. McDonald, *Bellevue,* 40.

11. Eastside Heritage Center Archives, Meydenbauer Collection.

12. Paul Dorpat, "A Candymaker's Home," *The Seattle Times,* February 2, 1987. McDonald, "Ah, Those Meydenbauer Yule Goodies," *The Seattle Times,* December 22, 1963.

13. Gaby Dickman, consultant in German for Lebkuchen recipe. Irma Rombauer, *Joy of Cooking,* (Indianapolis - New York: The Bobbs-Merrill Company, Inc., 1953 reprint), 687. "Honey, like molasses, is apt to be troublesome. Old German cooks used to insist on its being over a year old. Very good cakes are made with fresh honey but then the amount of flour is a little hard to gauge. . . ."

14. McDonald, *Bellevue,* 68.

15. Don Johnson interview by author, 4 August 2006. Plate meals (in the 1920's and 1930's sometimes called "Blue Plate Specials") were an inexpensive full meal, a daily special.

16. Mrs. Carter's Kitchen advertisement, The Lake Washington Reflector, 20 December 1927. "Philbrook House," Historic and Cultural Resources Survey, City of Bellevue 1993, #9.

17. McDonald, *Bellevue,* 77-79.

18. Mumford, *Calabash,* 137.

19. McDonald, *Bellevue,* 88, 105.

20. McDonald, *Bellevue,* 102

21. *Bellevue Chronicle - 1863-1990,* 3. McDonald, *Bellevue,* 85

22. Doug Margeson, "Traditions live at town's focal point," *Journal American,* 15 May 1995. *The Lake Washington Reflector,* 20 June 1919, 20 September 1923.

23. McDonald, *Bellevue,* 88. Kathleen Kardong, correspondence, 5 September 1995, Archives, Eastside Heritage Center.

24. "Fisher Flouring Mills officially opens on Harbor Island in Elliott Bay on 1 June 1911," <http://www.HistoryLink.org>, Essay 3927.

25. Fisher Mills Cookbook, "Cooking Recipes," Eastside Heritage Center Archives.

26. *The Lake Washington Reflector,* 1 January 1927.

27. Mike Intlekofer, correspondence, 2005. McConaghy, ed., *Lucile McDonald's Eastside Notebook,* 108-109.

28. Connie Beals, "Strawberries and sawmills: It was 1913 when Louis Aries decided to..." *Journal American,* 9 Sept 1977. The Aries Brothers operated an 80-acre truck farm from 1913 to 1960 near 156th where the K-Mart eventually locates. In 1918 they ship seven carloads of iceberg lettuce from Bellevue and produced more than 4,000 sacks of potatoes. Their produce shipped to the Midwest and even to Alaska. Refrigerated train cars: Brenner, *American Appetite - The Coming of Age of a National Cuisine,* 19.

29. Evelyn Hastings, "Blueberry Farm Built on Memories," *The Seattle Times,* 15 September 1957.

30. McDonald, *Bellevue,* 66.

31. *The Lake Washington Reflector,* 1 January 1924.

32. Knauss, ed., *A Point in Time,* 20.

33. "Farm Heritage," *Journal American*, 5 August 1990. *Bellevue American*, 20 February 1947. Historic and Cultural Resources Survey, #15.

34. "Memories of Living and Farming in Mercer Slough," Bellevue Historical Society Oral Histories Project, the Balatico and Smith Families, 13 March 1998, Eastside Heritage Center Archives. Ann Berglind and Karen Van Scholack, "Bellevue Potpourri," *Eastside à La Carte,* (Snohomish Publishing, 1980), 62. McDonald, Bellevue, 126.

35. Keiko Morris, "A Bellevue Man of the Soil sees more than just crops grow in past 50 years," *The Seattle Times,* August 20, 1997. Neiwert, *Strawberry Days,* 227. A personal recipe book: "Cooking Recipes," Eastside Heritage Center Archives.

36. Tsushima, Asaichi, "Pre WWII History of Japanese Pioneers in the Clearing and Development of Land in Bellevue", 1952, Eastside Heritage Center Archives.

37. Neiwert, *Strawberry Days,* 89 - 90. Note: one of the original vegetable cooperative buildings still stands in the Midlakes area, today a window and household glass business. "New Strawberry to Bring Better Price to Grower," *Eastside Journal* (Kirkland, WA) 1 March 1923.

38. Mitzie (Takeshita) Hashiguchi, interview by author, 17 May 2005. Valerie
Winslow, "Bellevue Strawberry Festival: Gone but not forgotten," *Journal
American,* 24 July 1975.

39. Seattle visitor Gloria Nourse, penned this poem as reported in *The Lake
Washington Reflector,* 20 June 1925.
    We have wandered from the city
    In search of a new thrill,
    We found a place so pretty
    That we stuck around until
    We filled up on Strawberries,
    Shortcake and lovely cream
    The berries red as cherries,
    The shortcake just a dream.
    It was the town of Bellevue.
    A little rustic place
    Where all this classy food grew
    To feed our hungry face.
    We thank thee little township
    We like your Festival.
    When'er we make a short trip
    Upon you we will call

40. Stein and the HistoryLink Staff, *Bellevue Timeline,* 28. McDonald, Bellevue,
113.

41. Karolevitz, *Kemper Freeman, Sr. and the Bellevue Story,* 40.

42. Jim Ditty, "When the Strawberry was King," *The Observer,* 1965.

43. Evelyn Hastings, "Blueberry farm built on memories."

44. *Historic and Cultural Resources Survey,* #41 Larsen Lake.

45. *Historic and Cultural Resources Survey,* #40 Overlake Blueberry Farm. Bill

Pace, interview by author, 9 August 2005.

46. McKean, *Pacific North West Flavors.*

47. Sydnor's recipe for Blueberry Buckle, a simple old standard with the improbable name, really produces a coffeecake. The berries collapse, or "buckle," into the batter as it bakes; hence, the name.

48. Penny O'Byrne, interview by author, 2005. "History of the Overlake Service League," 1911-1959, Overlake Service League Archives. *The Lake Washington Reflector,* October 1918, Eastside Heritage Center Archives.

49. "History of the Overlake Service League." Rombauer, *Joy of Cooking,* 725.

50. Pete Hogue, "Old Bulb Farm Falls to Progress," *Daily Journal American,* 1960's. Eastside Heritage Center Archives. Eastside Heritage Center Archives, Delkin Bulb Farm file.

51. Trish Carpenter, Overlake Service League Past President, Chair Fundraising Projects 2003 to 2006, interview by author, 2005.

52. Donna Jean Perry, interview by author, 28 June 2005. Bellevue Historical Society Oral History Project interview with Phyllis Fenwick, 6 November 1989. The Lake Washington Reflector, 10 February 1921. The Cruse-Hill families lived in the Baker House circa 1912.

53. *The Lake Washington Reflector,* 29 June 1933.

54. *Greater Bellevue Washington,* 57. Highland Literary and Improvement Club 1910-1912 records, Eastside Heritage Center Archives. In the 1930's, the Grange enjoyed card parties and dances at the Highland Clubhouse. *The Lake Washington Reflector,* 2 November 1933 and 29 June 1933.

55. McDonald, *Bellevue,* 124-125.

56. *The Lake Washington Reflector,* 20 February 1927, and 10 July 1927. Note: at one time a road led up to the Wake Robin Inn, at 108th SE and SE 23rd, from Bellevue Way.

57. Leila Martin and William B. Cook, Oral Histories, "Wake Robin Inn," Janu-

ary, 2006. Eastside Heritage Center Archives. Mumford, *Calabash,* 136.

58. "The Beacon," 1933 Overlake High School Annual. Eastside Heritage Center Archives.

59. Fran Bigelow, interview by author, May 16, 2005. Bigelow, *Pure Chocolate,* (2004), 3.

60. Diana Schafer Ford interviews by author, 11 October 2004 and 7 February 2005. Lucile McDonald, "Rationing," *Journal American*, 11 June, 1979. Donating sugar ration coupons required after 5 May 1942. In 1914,Woodrow Wilson declared Mothers Day a national holiday.

61. Monte Enbysk, "Such Sweet Sorrow," *Journal American,* August 1991.

62. Charles LeWarne, correspondence with author, 4 May 2006.

63. Reda and Paul Vander Hoek, interview by author, 15 February 2005. "Every Housewife Needs a Recipe Box," *The Lake Washington Reflector,* January 21, 1932.

64. Mary Barton, interview by author, June 2005.

65. Annie Stevenson, correspondence with author, 3 October 2006.

66. McDonald, *Bellevue,* 58.

67. Mitzie (Takeshita) Hashiguchi, interview by author, 17 May 2005.

68. Patricia Sandbo, interview by author, 2005.

69. Bellevue Woman's Club File, Eastside Heritage Center Archives. <http://www. womenshistory.com>.

70. King County Library Staff, information to author, 2005.

71. Heritage Personal Cookbooks, Eastside Heritage Center Archives. "Cooking Recipes," Eastside Heritage Center Archives.

72. Emmett Murray, "Bellevue Library has seen share of reincarnations," *The*

Seattle Times, 1 July 1993. "Librarian Lauds Early Use of Library Service," *Bellevue American,* M. Groves - Guest Cook, 26 March 1958.

73. Robere Le Huquet, grandson of Eugene LeHuquet, phone and e-mail correspondence with author, September, 2006.

74. Lucile McDonald, "Small Town Printer was Important Figure," *Journal American,* 23 July 1979.

75. *The Lake Washington Reflector,* 6 August 1931.

76. *The Lake Washington Reflector,* 27 September 1934.

77. *The Lake Washington Reflector,* 8 December 1932.

78. *The Lake Washington Reflector,* 18 October 1934.

79. *The Lake Washington Reflector,* 14 December 1933.

80. "U.S. Peppermint Oil in Demand," *The Lake Washington Reflector,* 1 November 1934. "Crescent Manufacturing Company," Essay 2006, <http://www.HistoryLink.org> Crescent Foods, the Seattle spice firm, began in 1883. Alan Stein, correspondence, 12 September 2006.

81. Ruby Erven, 25 September 2006, information to Robere Le Huquet.

82. "Homemade in the Kitchen," <http://www.recipelink.com>, 25 October 2006.

83. King County Library Research Librarians supplied newspaper founding dates.

84. Greg Atkinson, correspondence with author, 2005.

Food for Gracious Living 1940 to 1970

1. McDonald, *Bellevue,* 63, 73 - 77. Essay 2040, <http://www.HistoryLink.org>.

2. McDonald, Bellevue,134. Karolevitz, *Kemper Freeman, Sr. and the Bellevue Story,* 64-66. Banquet Menu, EHC Archives.

3. *Greater Bellevue Washington,* 1.

4. Stein and the HistoryLink Staff, *Bellevue Timeline,* 46.

5. Stein and the HistoryLink Staff, *Bellevue Timeline,* 8.

6. *Greater Bellevue Washington,* 3.

7. Village Inn Menu, Eastside Heritage Center Archives.

8. *Greater Bellevue Washington,* 11, 14, 65, 78, 91. *Bellevue-Kirkland City Directory,* 1959: The Barb, Kingen's, The Hut, Kandy Kane Kafe, Pancake Corral, Toy's Café, Village Inn and Clark's Crabapple are listed. Charlie Mitchell, growing up in 1960's Bellevue, remembers that as an annual tradition his family went to the Crabapple Restaurant for a special dinner. Several times a year they ate out at the Barb located in the Ditty Building near NE 8th on Bellevue Way. Occasionally, he was taken to eat lunch in the tearoom at the Bellevue Frederick & Nelson where they served a milkshake in a metal container.

9. Photo: Annie (Joanne Mermod) Stevenson, correspondence with author 4 November 2006. Florence Christiansen, class of 1948, stands behind the round table.

10. Grindeland, *Art: A Fair Legacy,* 6, 7, 10.

11. Patricia Sandbo interview by author, 15 February 2007. Recipe courtesy Patricia Sandbo.

12. Speidel, *You Can't Eat Mount Rainier,* 28.

13. 1958 Photo: clockwise from top left Harold Silkett (Uncle Harold's Key and Cycle Shop), Don Helberg (*Bellevue American*), Don Clark (CPA), Lib Tufarolo (Mayor Clyde Hill), Wes McKenzie (Optometrist), Hart Rutledge (Pacific National Bank), Carol Barber, Bob Reilly (Bellevue Playbarn Veteran).

14. Information on Carol Barber: Maxine Behrman, Historian Meydenbauer Bay Yacht Club Archives.

15. "Pancake Day Proceeds to Benefit Hospital," *Bellevue American,* 26 February,

1959.

16. Ada Williams, interview by author, 13 May, 2005.

17. Sherry Grindeland, "Arthur's last loaf," *Journal American,* 24 March 1994. Arthur, Elaine and Steve Wilk, interview by author, 23 February, 2005. Note: in 1956 another on-site bakery, The Dainty Maid, existed on Main Street, but by 1959 had closed and moved to Seattle. The Milk Barn, a drive-through bakery, also sold bread then, offering four loaves for a dollar, but they soon went out of business.

18. Karolevitz,, *Kemper Freeman Sr. and the Bellevue Story,* 87-89.

19. Betty Freeman, interview by author, 29 April 2005.

20. Barbara Catt, correspondence with author, 22 November 2006.

21. Spector, *The Legend of Frango Chocolate,* 3,18.

22. Spector, *The Legend of Frango Chocolate,* 29-30.

23. Spector, *The Legend of Frango Chocolate,* 12.

24. Courtesy Toni Keene, Bon Marché Food Consultant, 2005.

25. Jorge Valls in Nordstrom's Corporate Public Relations and Valerie Ripp at the Bellevue Nordstrom Concierge, 2005. Stephanie Eby, 29-30 January 2007. Elmer J. Nordstrom, *A Winning Team - The Story of Everett, Elmer & Lloyd Nordstrom,* private publication, 1985. Frank McCaffrey, *John W.Nordstrom: The Immigrant in 1887,* (Dogwood Press, 1950). In 1901 John W. Nordstrom, a Swedish immigrant, came to Seattle with $13,000 earned in an Alaska gold mine stake. He became reacquainted with Carl Wallin, who had also been in Alaska and had a shoe repair store on 4th Avenue. Soon they opened the Wallin & Nordstrom Shoe Store. By 1928, Wallin had sold his share of the business to Nordstrom and his sons. The corporation now operates 151 U.S. Nordstrom stores in 27 states.

26. Marilyn Goesling, interview by author, 23 May 2005.

27. McDonald, *Bellevue,* 84-85.

28. Nat Green, interview by author, 15 January, 2006.

29. <http://www.pigglywiggly.com>.

30. Lucile McDonald, "James Ditty - one of Bellevue's earliest developers," *Journal American,* 17 September, 1979, East Side History. City of Bellevue, *Bellevue Chronicle 1863 - 1990,* 7.

31. Kirsten Maas, correspondence with author, 13 December 2006.

32. Jim Wire, interview by author, 8 September 2006.

33. Grindeland, *Art: A Fair Legacy,* 4.

34. Grindeland, *Art: A Fair Legacy,* 65, 85, 108-109.

35. "Blueberry Festival This Week," *Bellevue American,* 26 July, 1951. "Blueberry Pies, Tarts, Muffins Sell out Fast," *Bellevue American,* 2 August, 1951, 1. Arthur Wilk Family, interview with author, 23 February, 2005. East side Heritage Center Archives: Bellevue's blueberries made news in the "other" Washington when Chamber of Commerce President Herbert Metke sent Senator Magnuson a blue berry pie to give to President and Mrs. Eisenhower. Their enthusiastic thank you letter survives as a testament to the farming enterprises that gave initial life to the community.

36. Yvonne Miller, Past President Pacific Northwest Arts and Crafts Association Board and Fair Chairman, interview by author 25 March 2005. "Food, Refreshments Have Their Part at Arts and Crafts Fair," *Bellevue American,* 23 July, 1970.

37. "Northwest salmon will be the 'specialty of the house' at the traditional Indian barbecue served during the three days at the Arts and Crafts Fair in Bellevue Square. This year three Overlake Memorial Hospital Auxiliaries will join the four PANACA (Pacific Northwest Arts and Crafts Association) foundation units to present the barbecue dinner which will also include barbecued chicken. Three members of the participating OMH auxiliaries join in the barbecuing discussion as menu plans are made, from left: Mrs. Don Hibbard, Mrs. Ralph Clark, Mitchell Wolfe of Byron's Country Kitchen, where the food will be prepared, Mrs. Robert Baker and Mrs. Charles Scott, chairman of the barbecue dinner."

38. Gail Glasgow, Director Arts & Crafts Fair, correspondence with author, 2005. Elisabeth Wahlers, Director Bellevue Arts & Crafts Fair and Renate Raymond, Director External Affairs, correspondence 14 February 2007 and 20 February 2007.

39. Grindeland, *Art: A Fair Legacy,* 11.

40. Author notes on the event, 26 July 2006: The cocktail served, a pomegranate Manhattan, reflects the current popularity of "healthy" foods. Antioxidants in pomegranate juice supposedly counteract the effects of alcohol.

41. Arlene Alton, BAM docent, correspondence with the author, 26 July 2006.

42. Lin Salisbury, correspondence with author, 6 January 2006. In addition to baking lots of cookies and appetizers for community causes since the 1960's, Lin Salisbury served as a trustee for the Pacific Northwest Arts & Crafts Association and Bellevue Art Museum from 1967 to 1997 and as chair of the annual Arts and Crafts Fair in 1974 and 1981.

43. James McGrath, M.D., interview by author, July, 2005.

44. Lorraine Weltzien, Overlake Hospital Historian, interview by author, 25 February 2005. The Overlake Hospital Auxiliary fundraising recipe books reflect the availability of local seafood. Lorraine Weltzien remembers serving a lot of crab because it was so incredibly cheap. In 1955, the Bellevue Safeway sold Alaskan King Crab for 69 cents a pound.

45. Ontie Griebel, Director, Bandage Ball, Overlake Hospital, correspondence with author, 9 January 2007.

46. "Festive Feeds" Overlake Hospital Auxiliary cookbook. Charles Le Warne, correspondence with author, 24 January 2007.

47. Suzanne Hutchinson, interview by author, 9 August 2005. Cookie Exchanges, <http://www.robinsweb.com>, December 2005. Cookie exchanges in America, popular since the mid-years of the twentieth century, provide an opportunity to get together and share with friends at holiday celebrations.

48. "Norwood Village," *Living for Young Homemakers* (September 1952), Eastside Heritage Archives.

49. Norwood Village Wives, *Village Vittles,* 1.

50. Norwood Village Wives, *Village Vittles,* 104.

51. "Norwood Village," *Living for Young Homemakers* (September 1952).

52. Maxine Behrman, Historian for the Meydenbauer Bay Yacht Club, correspondence with author, 10 October 2005.

53. Jan Conrad, interview by author, 9 August 2006. Note: eventually, Overlake Hospital adopted the Cancer Link program for its patients.

54. Bob Hollister, General Manager Overlake Golf & Country Club, correspondence with author, 4 August 2006.

55. "Governor Honors 'Borgy,'" *Bellevue American,* 17 September, 1970. Joan Eck, "Hot-lunch program's founder looks back on big family," *The Seattle Times,* 20 September 1970, B12. <http://www.encarta.msn.com>, United States Great Depression years: 1929 to early 1940's. <Http://www.fns.usda.gov>. Harry Truman signed the National School Lunch Act in 1946.

56. Bellevue Schools Scrapbooks, PTA Hot Lunch, 12 October 1941, Eastside Heritage Center Archives.

57. Cathy Dumas, Nutrition Services Manager, Bellevue School District, interview by author, 6 March 2007.

58. Penny O'Byrne, interview by author, 2005. Records Overlake Service League. *The Lake Washington Reflector,* October 1918, Eastside Heritage Center Archives. Trish Carpenter, interview by author, 2005. Cathy Dumas, Nutrition Services Manager, Bellevue School District, telephone interview by author, 6 March 2007.

59. Nancy Jones, interview by author, 14 March 2007. Shelley Noble, correspondence with author, 1 March 2007.

60. Mitzie Hashiguchi, interview with author, 17 May 2005 and 9 August 2006.

61. Irene Leggate, interview with author, 19 January 2006.

62. Kristi Weir, interview with author, 2005, and correspondence 3 February 2007.

63. Bellevue-Issaquah Pacific Telephone Directories for 1958 and 1959, Seattle Public Library., Note: no listing appears for Toys in the 1958 directory; it is listed in the 1959 directory. *The Lake Washington Reflector,* "Younger Purchases Bus Terminal," 1 May 1929. Map, Eastside Heritage Archives. Nat Green, interview with author, January, 2006.

64. Pamela S. Leven, "Going, Going (Arden in State Gone)," *Seattle Post-Intelligencer*, 8 June 1979, Business/Marine p C12, col. 1. Arden operated in Seattle for "over 50 years." Arden, originally a small California dairy operation, appears in the Polk's Seattle City Directory in 1935, located at "1501 4th Ave S at Atlantic." According to the *P-I* article, Arden was "one of the first to develop wide acceptance for ice cream. . . ."

65. Anna Hon, correspondence with author, 31 October, 2006.

66. McDonald, *Bellevue,* 101.

67. Sherry Grindeland, "Burger joint lures high-tech fans," *The Seattle Times,* 1 September, 2000.

68. *Great Bellevue Washington,* 78.

69. Martha Kingen, interview and correspondence with author, 20 January 2006. Gerry Kingen sold the Red Robin to Japanese investors, but continued with his brother, Larry, to design and open new Red Robins.

70. Gene Morley, interview by author, 5 April 2006.

71. Ron Schmeer, correspondence with author, 18 September 2006. Jack Alton, interview by author 12 July 2006.

72. Dick Spady, interview by author, 19 July 2006. *Bellevue American* 10 August 1967. Company President Dick Spady developed his business principles in Bellevue, first at the Forum Foundation and later at Dick's. He believed in the concept of building sustainable communities and that successful businesses have a responsibility to their communities.

Diversifying Food Traditions 1970 to 1990

1. McDonald, *Bellevue,* 159.

2. "Julia Child Will Demonstrate Her Famed Culinary Techniques," and Stan Reed, "Just Think of the Leftovers" *Seattle Post-Intelligencer*, 16 November 1971.

3. Garreau, *Edge City.*

4. Brenner, *American Appetite,* 25, 29, 44-47, 49.

5. "Julia Child Autograph Party and Cooking Demo," *Seattle Post-Intelligencer,* 16 November 1971.

6. <http://www.williams-sonoma.com>.

7. Nancy Lazara, interview by and correspondence with author, 4 October 2005 and 30 January 2006.

8. Saint Marks News Release, 1974: MOHAI Archival Files.

9. Nancy Lazara, interview by author. Janet Brandt, "Make her's *[sic]* with Berries," Section B, Living, *The Daily Journal-American,* 9 June 1978. Alf Collins, "Chef effects change in supermarkets' content and intent," *The Seattle Times,* 18 June 1986.

10. Jeannette Sullivan, interview by author, 5 February and 16 May 2005.

11. Jeannette Sullivan, interview by author.

12. Debbie Jaffe, interview by author, 4 May 2006.

13. Sharon Kramis, interview by author, 13 January 2007. Portland native James Beard's cookbooks and articles in *Gourmet* magazine promoted regional cuisines and wines.

14. Ingle and Kramis, *Northwest Bounty,* 267. Kramis, Berries, 76.

15. Hillary Benson, Communications Manager, correspondence with author 18

July 2005. Nicole Johnston, correspondence with author 27 February and 31 March 2007. Cookbooks: Junior League of Seattle, *Celebrate the Rain or Simply Classic,* <http://www.jrleagueseattle.org>.

16. Root and de Rochemont, *Eating in America,* 419 and 423-427. In the nineteenth century, sodas and sundaes became popular. The Evanston, Illinois, Women's Christian Temperance Union campaigned for sodas as an alternative to alcohol. Prohibition (1920 - 1933) encouraged the switch from spirits to ice cream desserts purchased at the soda fountain.

17. Kamp, *The United States of Arugula,* 191-192.

18. "Frozen Nostalgia," *Newsweek,* 26 July, 1971, Volume LXXVIII, 53. David Kamp, *The United States of Arugula,* 191: In the 1970's, premium ice cream manufacturers, notably Ben and Jerry's and Steve Herrell, brought ice cream making back to its higher butterfat origins. Roger Baker, "Where Can Farrell's Go?" 2006, <http://www.happyitis.biz/History>. Farrell's Reminiscences, Chuck LeWarne, 15 February 2007.

19. Paul Jaffe, interview with author, 11 January 2006. Note: Earle Swensen opened his first shop in 1948 in San Francisco, known as Swensen's Old Fashioned Ice Cream shop. It still exists, located at Union and Hyde. "Best of San Francisco, Food & Drink, 2005, Best Ice Cream Shop," <http://www.sfweekly.com>.

20. Kyle D. Fulwiler, correspondence with author 16 May and 14 August 2006. Gail Round, correspondence with author 16 August and 11 September 2006. Kyle D. Fulwiler is the Chef at the Governor's Mansion in Olympia 1983 to present (2007). Gail Round is a Non-Public CPA in Bellevue. Both grew up in Bellevue.

21. Jean McClure, interview with author, 18 January 2006.

22. Christine Muhlke, "Quest for Fire: Satisfying a Primitive Dessert Urge," *The New York Times Style Magazine,* Spring 2006, 98. Girl Scout camping pamphlets as early as 1927 describe S'Mores.

23. Williams, *The Way We Ate,* 169.

24. Karolevitz, *Kemper Freeman Sr. and the Bellevue Story,* 43.

25. Lucile McDonald, "Grapes," *The Journal American,* 30th April 1979. McDonald, Bellevue, 115.

26. Robert Hennig, Oral History, Eastside Heritage Archives.

27. Robert Hennig, interview by author, 26 January 2007. Robert Hennig helped prune the Borg's vines.

28. "Domestic wines" Newsweek, 7 June 1965, 67. "Vive le Brand X," *Newsweek,* 15 April 1974, 70. Andries de Groot, Roy, "What Can You Do About the Soaring Price of Wine? *Esquire,* January 1974, 111.

29. George Kingen, interview by author, 30 January 2007. By the end of the twentieth century, wine became a billion dollar industry in Washington State and its fastest growing sector of agriculture.

30. In the twenty-first century, Washington State is the second largest producer in the U.S. with more than 350 wineries, <http://www.washingtonwine.org>.

31. Tom Cottrell, interview by and correspondence with author, 22 July 2006 and 25 January 2007. Richard Kinssies "On Wine: 30 years of Chateau Ste. Michelle," *Seattle Post-Intelligencer*, 6 September 2006. Note: a wine-making shop also existed in Bellevue.

32. Paul Thomas, correspondence with author, 30 March 2006 and 2 May 2006.

33. Dorene Centioli McTigue, interview by and correspondence with author, 8 September 2006.

34. Peter Dow, interview by author, 5 May 2006.

35. The DeLaurentis, interview by author, 6 March 2006.

36. Joe Magnano, interview by author, 1 February 2006.

37. Lynn Rosenthal, interview by author, 7 December 2006

38. Charlie Brenner, telephone interview by author, 24 January 2005. Tina Anima, "A Brenner Reopening?" *The Seattle Times,* 8 January 1997.

39. Alan Kurimura, interview by author, 13 June 2006. Asians comprise close to 20 percent of Bellevue's current population.

40. Yoshi Yokomoyo, Yatsuko Nakajima, Office Manager, and Chef Masahiko Nakashima, interviews by author 18 January 2007.

41. Yoshi Yokomoyo, interview by author.

42. Gertrude Popp, interview by author, 21 September 2005 and correspondence with author, January 2007.

43. Beth Curtis, correspondence with author, 7 September 2006, and Gena Reebs, Communications Director, 16 January 2007. A group of local investors, headed by S.W. "Bill" Thurston underwrote the funding to build the club. Today, the Club has 5,000 memberships. The major enhancement was the opening in 1997 of a luxury hotel with 67 rooms.

44. Lynn Terpstra, Director Marketing, interview by and correspondence with author, 9 September 2005, correspondence 1 December 2006. Angeldawn Sippo, manager, Coldstone, interview by author, 9 November 2006.

45. Usha Reddy Sources: interview by author, 27 October 2006. John Hinter-berger, *The Seattle Times* restaurant critic, "Southern Indian flavors come alive at Golkonda," *The Seattle Times* 5-11 October 1995. Penny Rawson, "New restaurants and later hours enliven Eastside Public Market," *Journal American,* April 1991. Alison Oresman, restaurant critic, "A Taste of India - Spices blend to make exotic delights at new restaurant," *Journal American,* 29 September 1995. The Reddys have lived on Mercer Island and in Bellevue since 1976 when Lakshma Reddy, now a retired Associate Professor in Immunology, came to the University of Washington. Hyderabade refers to the south-central city in India and its cuisine.

46. Susan Benton, Crossroads Mall Property Manager, correspondence with author 25 January 2007.

47. Shelley Noble, interview by author, 6 June 2005 and correspondence with author 25 January 2007. "The Food Bank is where we started. It remains a core service and need, but we give more than direct service to those who need it in Bellevue. We also have in place systems to alleviate poverty and affect public policy," says Shelley Noble, Director of Family and Emergency Services.

48. Nan Campbell, interview by author, 9 May 2005.

49. McDonald, *Bellevue,* 105.

50. McDonald, *Bellevue,* 101.

51. Stein and the HistoryLink Staff, *Bellevue Timeline,* 67-68.

52. Lee Springgate, interview by and correspondence with author, 2 May 2005, 10 January 2006. McDonald, *Bellevue,* 105.

53. Marie O'Connell, interview by author, 1 September and 29 November 2005. The City Council dedicated the formal garden in the northeast portion of the downtown park as "Marie's Garden" in recognition of Marie O'Connell's contributions to the City of Bellevue during her tenure as City Clerk 1982 to 1992.

History and Culinary Traditions 1990 to 2000

1.   Stein and the HistoryLink Staff, *Bellevue Timeline,* 80.

2.   Eastside Heritage Center Archives: An attempt to organize Bellevue Historical Society in 1966 only survived until 1969. Margot Blacker, interview with author, 18 January 2006. Note: ". . . I am pleased we were able to save and restore the Winters House as well as a few other buildings around the city."

3.   1987 Strawberry Festival Revival, Eastside Heritage Center Archives.

4.   Eastside Heritage Center Archives, *Historic Structure Report Frederick W. Winters House,* City of Bellevue, Washington, 22 November 1989.

5.   Kristen Sierra, Marketing Events Coordinator, The Rosalie Whyel Museum of Doll Art, correspondence with author, 17 February 2007. Shelley Helzer, Co-Director Rosalie Whyel Museum of Doll Art. correspondence with author, 14 March 2007. German Wooden Doll, 1820-40 and Antique Kitchen - 18 3/4" Maker Unknown from *The Rose Unfolds: Rarities of the Rosalie Whyel Museum of Doll Art,* Authors Rosalie Whyel and Susan Hedrick, 1996.

6. Anna Littlewood, correspondence with author, 15 March 2007. John Evelyn quote from *Agar to Zenry* by Ron Freethy. Anna Littlewood helped set up the Botanical Garden docent program and currently serves on its Board Development committee.

7. Iris Jewett, interview by and correspondence with author, 31 March 2005. Norm Hansen, photographs and information, 25 February and 17 November 2006.

8. Stein and the HistoryLink Staff, *Bellevue Timeline,* 88.

9. "Starbucks Coffee opens first store in Pike Place Market in April 1971." File 2075, <http://www.HistoryLink.org>.

10. Kristen Siefken, Lane Marketing (Tully's), correspondence with author, 21 December 2005, 4 February 2007.

11. Gillian Allen-White, correspondence with author 2005 and 5 February 2007.

12. Norris Bevan, interview by author, 10 May 2005.

13. Phil Bevan, correspondence with author, 18 May 2005.

14. Pat and Bill Baker, interview by author, 5 February 2007.

15. "I Met 'The Man' at Dixies," <http://www.seattledining.com>.

16. LJ Porter, interview and correspondence with author, 8 November 2006.

17. *Eastside YMCA Anniversary,* Winter 1993.

18. Judy Smith, Senior Director Community Development Seattle YMCA, correspondence with author, 3 August and 5, 13, 18 September 2006. "East meets west...," *Journal American,* 15 July 1992. Patricia Moir, "Nobody to chat with," *Journal American,* 9 January 1994. Kobe YMCA and YMCA of Greater Seattle, "Cross-Cultural Program" Annual Report April 1992 to March 1993. Sherry Grindeland, "East meets West in the Kitchen," *Journal American,* 15 July 1992.

19. Sarma Davidson, Liepaja Committee, correspondence with author, 8 Decem-

ber 2004 and 8 February 2006. Latvians living in the Seattle area maintain their traditions and language at the church and social hall built just
north of Northgate Shopping Mall.

20. Mark McKinney, Larry's Spokesman, correspondence with author, 14 March
     2006. Note: after the Yankee Kitchen closed, Nancy Lazara of Yankee Kitchen
     took over the Bellevue Larry's cooking classes from 1993 to 2002.

21. Sharon Linton, Communications Manager, Meydenbauer Center, correspon-
     dence with author, 1 and 6 March, 2006, 7 February 2007.

22. Carrie Van Dyck, correspondence with author, 8 and 20 November 2006; Ron
     Zimmerman, correspondence with author, 20 November 2006. The Herbfarm
     Restaurant.

With Food Comes Understanding 2000 to 2007

1.   Stein and the HistoryLink Staff, *Bellevue Timeline*, 41.

2.   50 Fest File, Eastside Heritage Center Archives.

3.   Anne Taylor, 50 Fest correspondences with author, 1 July 2005, 18 January
     2006.

4.   Former Mayor Connie Marshall, correspondence with author, 3 June 2005.

5.   Kemper Freeman, Jr., Women's University Club Address, 30 March 2006.

6.   "Lincoln Square," *The Seattle Times*, A6, 3 July 2005. Bellevue Downtown
     Association, "Vibrant Living in the Big Village," "Building Bellevue," *Bellevue
     Downtown*, Fall 2006. Warren Cornwall, "Pacific Northwest," *The Seattle
     Times Magazine*, 20 August 2004.

7.   Cynthia Breen, Westin Hotel Director Sales & Marketing, correspondence
     with author, 2 November 2005. Margo Shiroyama, correspondence with
     author, 21 March 2006.

8.   Suzanne Harrington, PACE, correspondence with author, 1 November 2006.

9.   New City Hall, notes by author, 20 May 2006.

10. Susan Harper, City Hall Grand Opening, correspondence with author, 5 and 22 May 2006. *It's Your City Hall,* City of Bellevue.

11. Mary Pat Byrne, Arts Specialist City of Bellevue, correspondence with author. City of Bellevue, *Bellevue It's Your City,* June 2006 6, 7; Sculpture, 1. Byrne administers the Bellevue Arts Commission's programs, managing public art projects and installations that now number nearly fifty since her tenure. Of Bellevue's official view of art, she says that as the Bellevue Council looks to the future, "They see Bellevue as a cultural hub for the Eastside and have set this as a goal."

12. Sherry Grindeland, *The Seattle Times,* 18 April 2006. 17 July 2006, courtesy Sherry Grindeland to use recipe for Culinary History publication. Since 1997 at *The Seattle Times,* Grindeland also worked from 1989 to 1996 for *Journal American* as columnist and an award-winning feature writer. She authored the Bellevue Art Museum 2003 publication, *Art: A Fair Legacy (The Journey from Fair to Museum: A History of the Bellevue Art Museum).*

13. Sherry Grindeland, *The Seattle Times,* 18 April 2006.

14. Rosanne Cohn, "A Matter of Choice," *Dining Out, Bellevue Spectrum,* April, 1978, 28.

15. Kamp, *The United States of Arugula,* 277.

16. Lori Taylor, interview by author, 18 January 2006.

17. Carol Dearth, interview by and correspondence with author, August 27, 2006.

18. Christopher A. Smith, "For Dearth, there's never too many cooks in the kitchen," *Bellevue Reporter,* 27 September -10 October, 2006, 16-17.

19. Carol Dearth, correspondence with author, 27 August 2006.

20. David Hulbert, Whole Foods, correspondence with author, 22 August 2006. Erin Couch, Landis Communications Inc. (LCI), correspondence with author, 15 November 2006.

21. J.J. Johnson, correspondence with author, 16 November 2006.

22. Tatsuo Tomeoka, Store Manager, interview by and correspondence with author, 7 February 2007. Note: source, Tatsuo Tomeoka, matcha is produced from specially grown "*tencha*" (Heaven's Tea) leaves; matcha is ground into a fine powder after steaming, drying, and removing the leaf veins and stems. Koots uses only pure, certified-Organic matcha in all its matcha-based drinks.

23. Martin Fackler, "Sushi Is to Mrs. Paul's as Green Tea Lattes Are to...?" *New York Times,* Personal Business, Page One.

24. Tatsuo Tomeoka, correspondence with author, 8 February 2007.

25. Jean-Claude Ferré, correspondence with author, 2005.

26. Fran Bigelow interview by and correspondence with author, 16 May 2005 and 16 February 2007. Bigelow, *Pure Chocolate,* 2.

27. Bigelow, *Pure Chocolate,* 3.

28. Fran Bigelow, interview by author, and *Pure Chocolate,* 4, 170.

29. Joe Vilardi, interview by author, 10 February 2007. Bis is pronounced "beess" and means two in French, referring to the two original restaurant owners.

30. John Howie, correspondence with author, 28 February 2007.

31. Brynn Watanabe, "What Do Strawberries, Japanese Americans and Diversity Have to Do with Bellevue" 8th Grade Essay Contest Winner, 2003 Strawberry Festival Bellevue, Washington.

Bibliography

Batdorf, Carol. *Northwest Native Harvest.* Surrey, B.C.: Hancock House, 1990.

Bigelow, Fran, with Helene Siegel. *Pure Chocolate.* n.p.: Broadway Books - a Division of Random House, 2004.

Brenner, Leslie. *American Appetite: The Coming of Age of a National Cuisine.* New York: Perennial, 1999

Ficken, Robert E. and Charles P. LeWarne. *Washington: A Centennial History.* Seattle: University of Washington Press, 1988.

Garreau, Joel. *Edge City: Life on the New Frontier.* New York: Doubleday and Co., 1991.

Greater Bellevue Washington. Yakima, WA: Republic Publications, n.d. (estimated 1957).

Grindeland, Sherry. *Art: A Fair Legacy (The Journey from Fair to Museum: A History of the Bellevue Art Museum).* Bellevue, WA: Bellevue Art Museum, 2003.

Ingle, Schuyler and Sharon Kramis. *Northwest Bounty.* New York: Simon and Shuster, 1988.

Kamp, David. *The United States of Arugula: How We Became a Gourmet Nation.* New York: Broadway Books, 2006.

Karolevitz, Robert F. *Kemper Freeman, Sr. and the Bellevue Story.* Mission Hill, SD: The Homestead Publishers, 1984.

Knauss, Suzanne, ed. *A Point in Time: A History of Yarrow Point, Washington.* Bellevue, WA: Belgate, 2002.

Kramis, Sharon. Berries: *A Country Garden Cookbook.* San Francisco: Collins Publishers, 1994.

McConaghy, Lorraine, ed. *Lucile McDonald's Eastside Notebook.* Redmond, WA: Signal Graphics Printing, 1993.

McDonald, Lucile. *Bellevue: Its First 100 Years.* Bellevue, WA: Bellevue Historical Society, 2000.

McKean, Lori. *Pacific Northwest Flavors: 150 Recipes From the Region's Farmland, Coastline, Mountains & Cities.* n.p.: Clarkson Potter, 1995.

Mumford, Esther Hall. *Calabash: A Guide to the History, Culture and Art of African-Americans in Seattle and King County, Washington.* Seattle: Ananse Press, 1993.

Neiwert, David A. *Strawberry Days: How Internment Destroyed a Japanese American Community.* New York: Palgrave MacMillan, 2005.

Orchid, Christina. *Christina's Cookbook: Recipes and Stories from a Northwest Island Kitchen.* Seattle: Sasquatch Books, 2004.

Root, Waverley and Richard de Rochemont. *Eating in America: A History.* New York: Ecco Press, 1976.

Spector, Robert. *The Legend of Frango Chocolate.* Kirkland, WA: Documentary Book Publishers Corp., 1993.

Speidel, William C. *You Can't Eat Mount Rainier.* Portland, OR: Binfords & Mort., 1955.

Stein, Alan J. and the HistoryLink Staff. *Bellevue Timeline.* Seattle: HistoryInk/ HistoryLink, 2004.

The Lake Washington Reflector. Bellevue, WA, 1918 - 1934.

Williams, Jacqueline. *The Way We Ate: Pacific Northwest Cooking, 1843-1900.* Spokane, WA: Washington State University Press, 1996.

Index